Professor Birdsong's

157 Dumbest Criminal Stories

Leonard Birdsong

Winghurst Publications

Professor Birdsong's 157 Dumbest Criminal Stories
by Leonard Birdsong

ISBN: 978-0-9898452-2-9 (paperback edition)

Winghurst Publications
1969 S. Alafaya Trail / Suite 303
Orlando, FL 32828-8732
www.BirdsongsLaw.com
lbirdsong@barry.edu

Disclaimer:
The facts that are recounted in the stories in this volume are true and in the public domain, as best as Professor Birdsong can determine from his research of court documents, newspapers, and wire services. The author's commentaries on these stories are his own views and opinions and do not reflect the official policy or position of any Law school, Law firm or other organization with which the author may be affiliated. The opinions provided herein are not intended to malign or defame any religion, ethnic group, club, organization, company, individual or anyone or anything. The author further covenants and represents that the work contains no matter that will incite prejudice, amount to an invasion of privacy, be libelous, obscene or otherwise unlawful or which infringe upon any proprietary interest at common law, trademark, trade secret, patent or copyright. The author is the sole proprietor of the work and all parts thereof.

Permissions:
Cover graphic: © Ievgen Melamud | Dreamstime.com
Book cover design: Rik Feeney / usabookcoach@gmail.com

TABLE OF CONTENTS

Introduction - 5

Chapter One - 7
Dumb Criminals from Around the United States

Chapter Two - 34
Florida Dummies

Chapter Three - 42
Dummies from Abroad

Chapter Four - 53
A Few Drunken Dummies

About the Author - 61

Ordering Information - 63

Other books by Professor Birdsong - 65

Introduction

Professor Leonard Birdsong lives in Orlando, Florida where he teaches Criminal Law, White Collar Crime, Evidence, and Immigration Law. He has written many scholarly legal pieces since joining the legal academy.

Among his scholarly pieces are his articles entitled: Felony Murder: A Historical Perspective; and Comity and Our Federalism in the Twenty-First Century: The Abstention Doctrines. This is not one of those scholarly pieces! This volume takes a humorous look at crime and criminals.

Although he has been involved in serious criminal law work over the years as a prosecutor, a defense attorney, and a law professor, Professor Birdsong knows that it is good to get a good laugh at least once every day. That is why several years ago he began to collect and edit from the wire services and newspapers zany criminal law stories and stories about dumb criminals. He began posting the stories on his blog that was read by his criminal law students.

Years ago, as a young federal prosecutor Professor Birdsong was not opposed to arguing to trial juries that the defendant was dumb – and that is why he was caught. Often criminals are dumb. Sometimes they are so dumb it is funny.

This little volume contains 157of Professor Birdsong's funny stories about dumb criminals of the many he has collected over the years. The stories are all true. This volume will prove to you that there are truly some real criminal dummies out there.

Professor Birdsong hopes that you will get a few good laughs from this collection of dumb criminal stories.

Enjoy!

Chapter One

Dumb Criminals from Around the United States

If one looks hard enough it is not difficult to find that there are lots of dumb criminals in the world. Let's start with some of my favorite dumb criminal stories from around the good old United States.

Would you say it was an A cup or a B cup sized condom? A cross dressing man in New York City snatched a purse from a 74 year old woman, but left behind a strange clue -- a condom filled with water that he had been using as a fake breast. The suspect, clad in a short denim skirt and black tube top, fled the scene in a car with two other transvestites. Police are checking the condom for fingerprint and DNA evidence.

Gosh, just how darn pathetic can the human condition get? A one legged prostitute was killed in Brooklyn after a John hit her over the head, causing her to fall backwards out of her wheelchair and slam her skull against a wall. Elizabeth Acevedo, 38, was found by police laying unconscious on the 13th floor of the building in which she lived. She died after being taken to the hospital. Acevedo, who lost her leg in an accident involving a train, had a rap sheet with 67 arrests for prostitution and drug charges. She wore a prosthetic leg, but also used a wheelchair. Police believe she may have being servicing a John who hit her on the head. No suspects have been found.

This was death by idiocy. He should have just eaten the cold cuts. A Mississippi man, Robert Davis, was fatally burned after breaking into a bar. While in the bar he attempted to cook himself some food but set the building on fire. He sustained severe burns in the fire and died two days later.

Yep, hard times all over. Police arrested a Charleston, WV, man who tried to rob a video store with an empty cheesecake box. Paul Parrish II, 43, of Charleston placed the box on the counter of the Movie Gallery with a note that said it contained a bomb. The clerk refused to give Parish any money and Parish ran out of the store. He was soon arrested and told police he needed money for gas and cigarettes.

This one sounds rather gay. A Fresno, California house burglar rubbed spices over the body of a sleeping man before using an 8 inch long sausage to slap the face of another snoozing resident. Antonio Vasquez fled but was caught in a nearby field after police found his wallet and ID in the victims' home. The sausage was eaten by a dog after Vasquez tossed it away.

A Washington, D.C. thief made it too easy for police. Not only did he leave a fingerprint behind – he left his whole thumb. He had made off with cash from a D.C. brothel but he left the key piece of evidence behind when a prostitute wrestled with him and the machete he was carrying sliced off his thumb. Police caught up with him at a hospital emergency room. OUCH!

A Pennsylvania bank robber was so furious when told that the tellers' tills were empty he threatened to file a complaint with management before fleeing. When the robber walked in, the tellers were on a shift change and waiting for their cash drawers to be filled. The indignant but hapless robber was caught 10 blocks away. "How dare they not have money for me to steal!"

It is best not to lie to the police! A Wisconsin man found this out the hard way that lying to the police can get you in deeper trouble. When the police pulled over the man's car, he gave them a fake name – unfortunately, it was the name of someone wanted for a homicide. When he found out, he gave police his true name. He said he lied to them because he had several outstanding warrants.

Calvin Morett, a 19 year old Saratoga Springs, NY, high school student was cited for disorderly conduct. His conduct? He showed up at his high school graduation dressed as a 6 foot penis. Officials report that Morett went to court where he stood erect, manned up and pleaded guilty to the charge. For his punishment he was ordered to write a letter of apology to his school.

We never knew beer could be so expensive! A Colorado brewery worker was arrested for allegedly stealing 570 rare and expensive beers from his employers at Avery Brewery Company. Adam James Dickenson, 26 worked at the boulder business for a few months last year and is accused of stealing beers worth $200 to $300, including brands like Duck Duck Gooze, Rogue Old Crustacean, and a case of Isabelle Proximus.

Yes, pleasure quickly turned to pain, but everyone lived. Two Fargo North Dakota men were simultaneously having sex with a woman when Ashley Hunter, 33, asked Orlando DeWitt, 37, to switch positions with him. Police report that when Dewitt refused to change positions it touched off a bitter argument that ended with Hunter stabbing his three-some buddy.

OK! You have been warned! Please be careful if you ever drive through the town of Missouri City, Texas. Why? The town has decided to charge a "crash tax" to motorist involved in accidents. The bill can run as high as $2,000 per wreck. The tax is meant to pay for emergency responders and only those drivers deemed responsible for collisions will be charged.

This guy must drive a really big SUV. In Pittsburgh Police report that Thomas Jones siphoned off more than $40,000 gasoline from his ex-boss – by swiping a company gas card and using it to buy 11,000 gallons of gas for himself and others. Jones was arrested in mid July after his former boss at BW Wholesale Florist, Mike Ulrich, caught him in the act. Ulrich stated that after he reported Jones's $43,695.16 in fraudulent fill ups, he spotted Jones gassing up again – and delivered him to the police.

This was one weird family reunion and we are still a bit suspicious about it. Stephanie Ramirez was working in a pizza parlor in Denton, Texas when a robber wearing a wig and sunglasses barged in and demanded cash. As Rameriz took money from the register a coworker tackled the robber knocking off his disguise – and revealing that the robber was Rameriz's father. Police say they do not think that Rameriz herself was in on the robbery.

Pictures from social networking web sites are cropping up in court. Online photos tripped up Joshua Lipton, a 20 year old Rhode Island college junior who was charged in a drunken driving crash that seriously injured a woman. Two weeks after his arrest, he attended a Halloween party dressed as a prisoner. The photos were later posted on Facebook. Prosecutor Jay Sullivan used the photos to paint Lipton as an unrepentant partier living it up while his victim suffered in the hospital. The judge found the photos depraved and sentenced Lipton to two years in prison.

Bird feed? A passenger on a flight from Guyana was charged with smuggling 13 finches into the U.S. to use in singing contests. Customs agents noticed bird feed in the luggage of Terrence McLean at JFK Airport. After searching McLean the agents found the birds hidden inside women's hair curlers. The Guyanese finches are thought to sing better than their American brethren. McLean admitted that he hoped to sell the birds, which he had captured in the wild. He was arraigned in Brooklyn federal court. Bird singing contests???

This from the "worst get away ever" file:Three men stole a recliner from a Goodwill store in Cookeville, TN, threw it in the back of their pickup truck and tried to speed off, but the vehicle was out of gas and it stalled in the parking lot. Police found the truck, the recliner and the perpetrators in the middle of their own personal gas crisis.

Professor Birdsong always used to tell his criminal clients to keep their mouths shut when in jail, but they never learn. Here is a case in point. Brian Orkiszewski, 49, from Long Island lost his house to his ex-wife in divorce proceedings and was arrested for plotting to kill the judge who gave the house away. Seems Orkiszewski, already in jail for failing to pay more than $30,000 in child support, was arrested after telling fellow inmates he was shopping for a gun for the planned hit. Orkiszewski told inmates he was furious that the house he had shared with his wife and three children had been awarded to his former spouse. Orkiszewski pleaded not guilty to conspiracy and criminal facilitation charges. His defense his attorney said Orkiszewski was, "frustrated, angry, and depressed." The judge in the original divorce proceedings was given court ordered protection.

A plea deal always saves the court money. Tremayne Durham, 36, of Portland Oregon was recently sentenced to life in prison with the chance for parole after thirty years. Durham was sentenced for the murder of Adam Calbreath over a business deal that had gone bad. Instead of going to trial Durham availed himself of a very unusual plea deal offered by the prosecutor. He had sat in jail almost two years awaiting trial and missed the greasy food he liked to eat. So, when the prosecutor offered him a fast food buffet in exchange for his guilty plea Durham admitted he had shot Calbreath. His buffet deal included gorging himself on KFC and Popeye's chicken, mashed potatoes, coleslaw, carrot cake, a pizza, two calzones, lasagna and ice cream. The judge signed off on the plea deal and Durham downed the food at two settings. Cost to the Oregon taxpayers was only $41.70. A murder trial would have cost the state $4,000.

The grammar police got policed! Two members of an Arizona group called the "Typo Eradication Advancement League" were arrested for defacing a historic, hand painted sign in the Grand Canyon by fixing grammatical errors on it. Both men were sentenced to a year's probation and cannot enter any national park. They must also pay $3,035 to repair the sign.

What a nincompoop! Federal agents in Montana were led straight to a man wanted for a fatal beating because he had his name tattooed on his head. That made it easy for the agents to find Sterling F. Wolfname – even though he tried to tell them he was somebody else.

Free videos? A Colorado man posing as a "porn inspector" tried to get the owners of an x-rated video shop to give him free videos, claiming he had to make sure performers were not under age. Of course, the local police when contacted by the video shop said they do not have a porn inspector. Go figure…

He lost by a nose. A cross-dressing bank robber donned a wig, makeup and women's clothing to throw police off the scent. Yet, he got caught because he could not disguise his large nose. Samuel Manoharan,31,of North Bergen, New Jersey, was arrested as a suspect in five bank robberies in Manhattan and Brooklyn because police were able to clearly identify him from his profile taken by bank surveillance cameras – namely his nose, sources said. "He has very distinguishable features – a very large nose. His wig couldn't cover his nose," said a police source.

A thug robbed an 81 year old widow in an Upper East Side grocery and nearly got away with the crime until he threw out his own wallet while trying to escape capture. Ex con Trent Jones, 26, of Manhattan swiped the elderly woman's wallet from her purse while an accomplice chatted her up about the tomatoes at the market. The pair fled after getting the wallet. The victim told the store owners of the theft. They gave chase. The fleeing Jones threw his own wallet on the sidewalk just before being caught by the store owners. Police were called. The wallet contained Jones' ID, as well as his victim's credit cards.

Torah, Torah, Torah…Police detectives believe the theft of eight Torahs – worth up to $400,000 – from a Queens, New York synagogue was an inside job. Bernard New, past president of the synagogue said not only was there no sign of a break in, but the thief had to use four keys to open the ark containing the Torahs, donated to the synagogue over the past 60 years. Temple officials said that there were three sets of keys at the synagogue. No arrest was immediately made.

They should have sold them on eBay when they had the chance! In follow up to the previous story, three weeks later police report that a cash strapped janitor swiped the eight Torahs valued at $400,000 from the Queens synagogue and hid the sacred scrolls in a friend's closet. Eric Giraldo, 23, who was a custodian at the synagogue, and his friend Alan Lozano, 28, were both charged with grand larceny and possession of stolen property. If convicted both men face up to 15 years in jail.

No robber and no robbery in this case – only a dumb crook. Police in Englewood, NJ report that a man called 911 and reported a robbery after a gas station attendant wouldn't give him his money back for an unopened box of condoms. Police charged Kadien Jackson, 21, with making a false report. Officials had responded quickly to the call on a Sunday night and found the gas station employee who fit the description of the robber given by the caller.

Creepy! An accomplished Long Island magician and photographer was recently charged with using hidden cameras to record women and girls as they changed costumes during photo shoots at his home. Robert Infantino, 50, who bills himself as Long Island's favorite magician was charged with three counts of unlawful surveillance after cops said he taped a mother and her two daughters, ages 10 and 14 at his home on July 22.

Hoist by his own petard. A man trying to shake down $500 from a Pizza Hut in Nevada outed himself by sending cell phone photos of the restaurant sign he stole that showed his license plate in the background. Of course, using the license number, police were able to track down the 23 year old man and arrest him. Dumb…

It might have been cheaper to keep her. A Washington State man was sentenced to 12 years in prison for attempted murder after admitting he lured his wife into putting her neck into a noose by telling her he had set up a Halloween haunted house in their garage.

Sean Jennings, 36, who freed his wife after she lost consciousness told her that hanging was "better than getting a divorce," according to police.

Mrs. Brown was just too young at heart. A Wisconsin woman allegedly stole her daughter's identity so she could go back to high school. Wendy Brown of Green Bay, enrolled in Ashwaubenon HS and joined the cheer-leading squad, attending practices and going to a pool party at the coach's house before she was caught. Brown was charged with felony ID theft.

Talk about a nut job and a pervert! A Wisconsin man says his religious beliefs stopped him from murdering and raping women…but that apparently didn't prevent him from breaking into their homes, stealing their underwear and sending them threatening notes. Christopher Sullivan, 43, is accused of sending some of the women pictures of decapitated Barbie dolls, along with messages that they would be likewise treated and "we will have your skull at our table of sacrifice."

Chicken as a deadly weapon? Do they serve chicken in prison? Bet he'll choke on it. Frederick McKaney of Michigan got into a fight with his mother and stabbed her with a fork. When a neighbor tried to help the mother McKaney hurled 10 pounds of frozen chicken at the neighbor. The poultry left the neighbor woman with a wound that required five surgical staples to close.

McKaney pleaded guilty to felonious assault and faces four years in prison.

Nope – not at all funny! A man in Kennewick, Washington thought it would be funny to stroll into a bank on Halloween dressed as a terrorist bomber, complete with fake explosives wrapped around his body. The police disagreed. The 39 year old man donned a white robe, turban and a very realistic-looking fake bomb when he walked into the U.S. Bank branch in Kennewick, only to be stopped by police on his way out and ordered to lay on the ground. Police said the man, who may face charges, thought it would be a funny gag. Ha!

No love in this one. We hope he will find love in prison. A Louisiana man who offered to help his girlfriend renovate her home landed in trouble with her – and the police too – when he used $10,000 worth of stolen cabinets for the job. He also used carpet that he had ripped up from another burglarized home.

We don't find this holy in any way. A man importing bottles labeled "holy water" from Canada at the Niagara Falls border crossing was arrested when a federal drug-sniffing dog got a whiff of the water. It turned out to be ketamine, an animal tranquilizer sometimes used as an illegal party drug.

If you kill someone do not, I repeat, do not write a song describing how you did it. Rico Todriquez Wright, a rap artist from Atlanta was sentenced to 20 years in prison after killing a man and then writing a rap song that detailed how he did it and calling the victim, Chad Blue, by name. "Chad Blue know how I shoot," rapped Wright in the song. And now, so does everyone else. Idiot.

Maybe it was easier to have sex inside the joint. A Kentucky inmate who escaped from prison returned later that same day – and pleaded with guards to let him back in. Chad Troy, 21, told police his family urged him to surrender because they feared for his safety. He said he immediately regretted running out the open prison door during a work detail. "I'm sorry about what I did," he said.

Not at all finger licking good! Bernard Wood, 33, of Lynchburg, VA, was convicted of burglary and grand larceny in Lynchburg after prosecutors linked him to the crime scene by a greasy fingerprint. Wood apparently ate some fried chicken during the break-in and left his prints on a juice bottle.

Mommy what's a "Whizzinator?" It can be said that these two Pittsburgh entrepreneurs were not a bunch of whizzes -- or were they? The two pleaded guilty in federal court for selling a device called a "Whizzinator" that helped cheaters pass drug tests. The device was a prosthetic penis, in various skin colors that came with a heating element and fake urine. NFL running back Onterrio Smith in 2005 was caught with one of the devices at an airport check point.

D'OH!! So dumb! Perhaps this guy wanted to get caught. A dummy of a bank robber in Chicago handed a teller a note – written on the back of his pay stub. The FBI was able to track him down easily when he left behind the note bearing his name and address. The dunderhead now faces 20 years in jail.

El Stupido. A bumbling thief was foiled while robbing an Oregon car wash when he dropped his gun and it broke apart mid-heist. An employee then drove him off by blasting him with a power washer. The wet dummy ran off, and still has not been caught.

Pimp! Working girls need God's love, too. A former director of the Ohio governor's faith based initiatives office was arrested for creating a Web site where Johns could post reviews of prostitutes. Authorities say Robert Eric McFadden also helped organize $10 raffles that offered an evening with a hooker.

They say this fellow was aquatically stupid. The Kentucky "bank" an armed robber tried to rob was actually the offices of the local water district, complete with payment windows. When the man demanded cash, he was told customers had to pay by check only. He fled empty-handed...and red-faced!

Career up in smoke! Her career up in smoke! A Williamsport, Pennsylvania teacher mixed her A-B-C's with some P-O-T, say police. Beth Camp, 52, her husband and son were arrested at their home with 72 pounds of marijuana worth about $350,000, police said. Camp had been a 25 year veteran of the Williamsport Area School District.

Sounds like he should have beaten up his father instead. An Iowa man was recently charged with trying to motivate his son to play football by giving him steroids. Police caught on when the 14 year old went into a rage and beat up his mother. Investigators found a syringe and 105 pills in the boy's bedroom.

How dumb can you get! A former employee of a funeral home in Walnut Ridge, Arkansas broke in one night and began setting up a meth lab in the basement in the middle of the night. Unfortunately for him, he forgot the sheriff's office was right across the street. Police noticed something was amiss when they spotted lights on and promptly arrested him.

It's a family affair...it's a family affair.....A Baltimore, Maryland man, his wife and his son allegedly took turns trying to stab police officers who were breaking up a fight among them. First, the son attacked the officers, and when he was subdued, the father took a run at them, police said. When they had subdued him, the wife grabbed the knife and allegedly took another stab. It was reported that none of the police were hurt. Yes, arrests were made.

A man walked into a Barnstable, Massachusetts police station asking for help getting out of a pair of handcuffs was arrested after cops realized he had several outstanding warrants. The man claimed his sister had put the cuffs on him at a children's birthday party. Of course, they removed the cuffs, arrested him and slipped on another set. Dumkopf!

Wonder whether he will be able to sugar coat this crime. Police say an Ohio teen ordered more than $37,000 worth of candy from an online store and tried to bill it to his former high school. Company officials grew suspicious and called police, who told them to send an empty box. When the teen took delivery, he was arrested.

OMG, what torture! A man held a woman hostage in Toledo for three days, and did nothing but read the Bible to her. Troy Brisport grabbed the woman off the street, handcuffed her, put her in an adult diaper and read nonstop to her. She escaped after he fell asleep. ZZZZZZZ…

Hey, there's a fine line between a frat prank and kidnapping – we think they crossed it. Four University of Virginia students were arrested after grabbing a random passer-by, tossing him in the trunk of a car and releasing him 12 miles away. The victim did not find it funny and pressed charges. The pranksters each received 90 days in jail. It was more than likely a fraternity prank said police. More like kidnapping we'd say.

Nothing new here. They always make Satan the scapegoat! An Arlington, WA woman accused of stealing $73,000 from the Arlington church where she worked said the devil told her to do it. "Satan had a big part in the theft," the woman said. Police and prosecutors can hardly wait until Satan takes the stand in his own defense.

Was the sex act missionary or doggie style? Jason Savage, 29, was sentenced to 90 days in jail for performing a sex act with a vacuum at a Saginaw, Michigan car wash. Appalled witnesses immediately called police. Savage pleaded no contest to indecent exposure. He has been ordered to submit to drug testing.

Did he pay for those "favors?" A Detroit Michigan man was charged with "receiving sexual favors" – from a vacuum cleaner. When a resident complained there were unusual deeds being perpetrated behind a car wash, police went to investigate. Sure enough, a man, whose

ID was not released was using the vacuum for a sexual partner. He was escorted to jail to cool off.

Talk about having a bad day! Some days a dumb criminal just can't catch a break. A man who robbed a Darien, Connecticut bank wrecked his getaway car and then took a bus and taxi home, only to find his roommate dead from an apparent suicide, said police. David Maksimik, 59, was arrested after he called 911 to get help for his friend. Unfortunately, responding police found the money from the bank robbery.

Professor Birdsong would advise all criminals to plan their escape route before committing a robbery. Here's one reason why: St. Louis police were able to stop the woman, who allegedly tried to shoplift $1,200 worth of goods from a store, when she got confused and kept trying to go out the automatic "in" door. She then became agitated which drew authorities' attention.

Sorry, sister, this is not a good deal -- Easter is over! Prosecutors in Baltimore have agreed to let a religious-cult member charged with starving her baby son to death withdraw her guilty plea if the child is resurrected. Ria Ramkissoon, 22, kept the boy's body packed in mothballs for months because she thought he would come back to life.

He doesn't have a leg left to stand on? When police arrested a Des Moines man for stealing an artificial leg, they confiscated the prosthetic limb and left him hobbling. Rogoberto Zarazua Rubio, who was fitted for the leg at a medical supply store, walked out to take it for a test spin and allegedly never returned to pay for it.

Here's another one. Go on.....say it.....The funeral home doesn't have a leg to stand on. Yuk, Yuk, Yuk. South Carolina officials have exhumed the body of a 6-foot-7 minister after hearing rumors that his legs were cut off because the mortician had ordered a coffin that was too short. After opening the exhumed coffin, police said only that "there were problems with the body," and criminal charges are expected.

A retired Harrisburg, PA, police chief said he was held up by "'the dumbest criminal in Pennsylvania," which may be an understatement. A 19 year old man is under arrest for allegedly robbing John Comparetto at gunpoint -- while the victim was attending a convention of narcotics cops in Harrisburg. After Comparetto gave up his money and cell phone, he and fellow conventioneers chased down the petty hood as he tried to escape in a taxi. He was placed under arrest.

We hope he's not as fussy about jail food! Lyndel Toppin, of Philly, was arrested after attacking his fiancé for making his meatball sandwich the "wrong" way. Toppin became furious "due" to the victim not placing the cheese on his hoagie correctly," according to a police report. He allegedly grabbed a knife and nearly chopped off one of the woman's fingers before sinking his teeth into her wrist.

What nerve they have! They say a biblical tide of anger swept through the parking lot of the Worcester, MA, courthouse when a man tipped over an eight-foot statue of Moses. Not surprisingly Brendan Pemberton had just left the DMV. He said he was furious that officials refused to renew his license unless he paid off a 20 year old speeding ticket. What nerve…

He already has the Scarlet letter on his hands. A 13 year old Peoria, IL, boy got an early jump on a life of crime when he robbed a bank in Peoria. Cops caught the boy red-handed -- literally -- several blocks away after a dye pack exploded and covered his hands with red ink. "It's the youngest suspect I can remember," said Sheriff Michael McCoy, a 40 year veteran of the police force. Prosecutors are discussing whether to charge the boy as an adult.

Live scorpions? A New York City man trying to smuggle rare tortoises into the United States got stopped by customs after he claimed that he was actually bringing in scorpions --- thinking they wouldn't get anyone's attention. "The package was labeled as containing 50 live scorpions." When it was mailed through JFK Airport, court documents said. But all an inspector found was "14 live leopard tortoises and one dead one." No sting…

There was no hole in his apology. A Chicago teen who robbed a Dunkin' Donuts had a pang of conscience and returned an hour later to give back the $167 he took and asked the clerk for a hug. Unfortunately, the clerk spoke little English and did not understand the apology. The Po Po charged the 17 year old thief with aggravated robbery.

Yeeewwww.....spit! This fellow should watch CSI reruns everyday while in the slammer. Police in La Crosse WI, tracked down a thief who stole a tavern's safe, thanks to DNA collected from the chewing tobacco spit he left behind at the scene of the crime. A fisherman found the empty safe washed up on a sandbar in Illinois.

Yeeewwww...baby shi........Baby needs new diapers...really needs new diapers! A couple strong armed their way out of a Spokane Safeway grocery store by punching out a security guard so they could make off with a pack of huggies, police said. The man yelled "sorry" as he hit the guard in the face, police, further said.

Seems when you gotta go, you gotta go. Two Yellowstone National Park employees were fired after committing a national outrage by urinating into the "Old Faithful" geyser -- an act caught on the web cam that streams video of the landmark's eruptions. The two were fired, fined and banned from the Wyoming park. It appears that criminal charges for UIP -- urinating in public were not filed.

He was a real "cereal" offender. Police in the Massachusetts town of Needham pulled over a man for driving erratically and discovered he was eating a bowl of cereal. When asked what he was doing the 48 year old driver replied, simply that he was hungry. Crunch…

You can run but you can't not steer! A handcuffed prisoner in Uniontown, PA who got away from police wrecked a truck he stole because he couldn't steer with his shackles on. Shaun Rosario escaped from a police car when it pulled over and the officer went to pay a toll. Police caught up with Rosario when he crashed.

A 66-year old Waukegan, IL, pilot was hit with a fine and given community service for landing his plane on an Illinois golf course so his 14 year old son wouldn't be late for his tennis lesson at a center next door. Robert Kadera had to pay a $500 fine and perform 60 hours of community service.

Bet this was one embarrassed dummy...I mean zombie. It doesn't pay to be the first zombie to arrive for a zombie convention. A man dressed in all black, knee pads, a gas mask and carrying what appeared to be a machine gun was the first guest at an event promoting the Crypticon Horror Convention in Seattle, but someone mistook him for a gunman and called police. A dozen police cars responded before someone realized the mistake. No arrest was made. Zombie convention? Why?

LOSER! Police in Portsmouth, NH had no trouble identifying this assault suspect -- they had arrested Paul Baldwin 152 times before. The 49 year old career criminal has a record dating back to 1984. His most recent bust came just days after he had completed a one year prison sentence for one of his previous crimes.

Bikini bandits, maybe? Surveillance cameras at a Lafayette, LA apartment complex captured two bikini clad pretty young girls stealing items from several cars parked outside. The klepto-chicks stole a GPS, a wallet and sunglasses, then fled on foot. Bet they wore teeney, weeney, polka dot bikinis...

No good deed goes unpunished. There's a fine line here between being a good Samaritan and a criminal nuisance. A man who took it upon himself to mow unkempt grass in a public park was arrested after police told him to stop and he refused. John Hamilton said he mowed only when the grass had gotten to be a foot high. Sandusky, OH, city officials say budget cuts have left them understaffed.

Old and dumb. Courtrooms can be such a drag some say. A Texas defense attorney was arrested in a hall of justice for allegedly carrying marijuana and a pipe in her purse. A security guard at the Bexar County, TX, Courthouse arrested Regina Criswell, 50, at a screening station. The dumb legal eagle told authorities she had been holding the contraband for a client.

Guys...bend over and spread 'em. A legal bordello in Nevada has announced it has hired male prostitutes to broaden its business. One problem is that although state law allows guys as well as gals to ply their trade, it also mandates cervical exams for all hookers.

Can we say he was living high on the hog? An upstate New York man and his alleged drug dealer were arrested in Fulton on narcotics charges after police saw an unusual trade. Angelo Colon allegedly bought a $50 bag of crack from Omar Velez for $10 -- and half a slaughtered pig! Velez told police he had planned to cook the pig to celebrate a relative's release from prison.

You're Out! This coach taught his players more than stealing bases. A Little League coach in Washington state has been accused of using some of his players to help him in a break-in. George Spady Jr. allegedly took his son, a nephew and another player from the team with him when he burglarized a store. He was charged with the burglary after one of the kids decided not to "play ball" and told his stepfather about the break-in.

....but did they find the printing press? An Alabama man might have had his last Big Mac for a while. The burger-lover was arrested for allegedly passing a phony $100 bill at a McDonald's in Madison, AL, leading police to find $16,000 more in counterfeit C-notes in his home.

Put that nasty thing away you pervert! Perhaps, it's all about easy access. An Oregon man had his pants custom tailored so he could easily flash young girls with less chance of being caught. Unfortunately for him, it did not work, and apparently, he had not learned his lesson. Byron Earl Huff, 47, has 21 prior arrests for public indecency, among other charges.

Hey nincompoops here's a great way to fight crime -- steal the thieves' getaway car. Patrick Rosario of Bellevue, WA, heard burglars breaking in to swipe his three flat screen televisions. Rosario, 32, sneaked out while calling 911 and saw the getaway van's motor running, keys in the ignition and no one inside. So Rosario drove off with the van to a friend's house, as the burglars fled on foot, leaving the TV's, a laptop computer and jewelry by his door.

Chapter Two

Florida Dummies

Professor Birdsong loves Florida. It is a great place to live. However, Florida does produce more than a few dumb criminals. This chapter comprises my favorite dumb criminal stories from Florida. That is why I call this chapter Florida Dummies.

It is sad that being a knuckle head in Florida seems to be spreading. Recently, a Florida man was arrested for making false 911 calls when he reported that a slot machine had "stolen" his money. That came two days after a man called 911 five times to ask for help settling an argument with his brother, and just a week after another Florida man called 911 to complain that a Subway sandwich shop had neglected to add condiments to his hero sandwich. Really dumb!

Doesn't sound like it took super-sleuthing to solve this case. Police did not have to look far to find this piece of stolen property. Dummies in Homestead broke into a rail yard and stole a 129 ton locomotive. Police were able to recover the behemoth seven miles away by following the track. The thieves were nowhere to be found.

Seems nothing is sacred any more… shame... shame… Jonathan Ricci, a Jensen Beach man, was arrested one recent Sunday morning after he allegedly tried to steal “a handful of communion wafers” from a priest at a Catholic church in Jensen Beach. During a 9 am mass, Ricci accepted a wafer in the Communion line, but walked away without taking it in his mouth. After a priest’s requests for him to accept the wafer, Ricci turned to the priest and grabbed a handful of wafers from the plate and attempted to leave St. Martin de Porres Church. Due to the religious significance of the

Holy Communion, a number of parishioners were upset at his callous treatment of their holy ritual and sought to detain him. An enraged Ricci then began to fight with two parishioners aged 82 and 66, respectively. They sustained minor injuries. Ricci was charged with theft, battery, and disrupting a religious assembly.

This Port St. Lucie student didn't understand that one is supposed to give an apple to their teacher -- not take it. An 18 year Port St. Lucie High School student allegedly swiped his teacher's decorative apple after the teacher confiscated a metal spring he was playing with during class.

Running with a cash register can be more dangerous than running with scissors. An Orlando man entered a Greenacres Restaurant in mid-July, and asked for change for a $10 bill. When the cashier asked to see the bill, the man reportedly began screaming, "I want change!" Police said the man then grabbed about $40 from a tip box, picked up the cash register and ran out. The officer who arrested him -- still carrying the register while running down the street -- had just come from reviewing surveillance footage at a nearby convenience store, where lottery tickets had been stolen a day earlier. By chance, the officer identified the man as the thief from the footage.

Yeah, right, the suit just slipped off... He's a perv. Lots of them hang out at water parks. A Connecticut man was arrested for exposing himself to a 14 year old girl at a Walt Disney World water park, swears it was because his "European-style" bathing suit slipped off. Witnesses told police that Bradford Pellet Biggers, 51, was fondling himself as he lay on a lawn chair about four feet from the girl. Perv!

Let's call him a "Minnie perv." A 60 year old man was convicted in August, of groping Minnie Mouse at Disney World. William Moyer of Cressona PA, claimed he was innocent of sexually assaulting the costumed park employee. But the victim testified in court that "she had to do everything possible to keep Moyer's hands off her breasts. Moyer was found guilty of misdemeanor battery. He must write the victim a letter of apology, serve 180 days probation, complete 50 hours of community service, pay $1,000 in court costs and undergo a mental evaluation.

Right, a mistake that the cat repeated 1,000 times! A man has been accused of downloading 1,000 images of child pornography. He blames his cat! Keith Griffin of Jensen Beach told investigators that his cat jumped on the computer keyboard while he was downloading music. It was all a mistake. Right…

Ewwwww… It's a crime against humanity to wear nothing but a banana hammock while riding on a bicycle banana seat in Florida. A 55 year old man known for riding a bike around Tallahassee wearing just a thong, and therefore frequently exposing himself, has been arrested. Richard Irby is notorious for walking around his trailer park with his genitals hanging from his skivvies.

A 34 year old wife was arrested in Fort Walton Beach for allegedly assaulting her husband after spotting him licking another woman's face. She dragged him out of a bar in Fort Walton Beach -- by his hair -- while hitting him.

CHEATER! A Tampa man triggered a manhunt after he lied to his wife about being kidnapped so he could be with his girlfriend, police said. Wikler Moran-Mora sent his wife a text telling her he had been abducted and was being held for ransom. Dummy…

OUCH! OUCH! HELP! YOW! DAMN! LORDY! OW! OW! WHUMP! Sylvester Jiles, who had been released days earlier from the Brevard County jail, decided he would be much safer inside after his life was threatened by people outside. So he tried to get back in by jumping the prison fence -- and fell through three levels of barbed wire. He was taken to a hospital.

And this is why we call it FloriDUH! Police in Fort Lauderdale sent letters to known fugitives promising them a "stimulus check" from the government. The suspects were asked to call a hotline and set up an appointment to pick up a check from an auditorium where "South Florida Stimulus Coalition" banners hung. When the fugitives arrived, they were identified and about 75 were arrested on offenses ranging from grand theft to fraud to attempted murder. Police say that the two day sting was dubbed "Operation Show Me The Money."

One gutsy burglar! A burglar who made off with a Pensacola man's valuables returned to the home later and snatched what he could not carry on his first trip -- a 100 pound plasma screen TV. The kicker to the story -- a police officer was on the scene investigating the first burglary when the thief made off with the TV. The owner of the house said the thief had already stolen his wallet, watch and video game system. Investigators had left the TV in the backyard, where the burglar put it, so they could dust for fingerprints. Police have offered to pay for the TV.

A woman broke into a car parked at a Fort Pierce police station to get change for the soda machine. Sophia Paulinyce, 19, was arrested for stealing $7 from a police officer's private vehicle and charged with felony burglary and misdemeanor larceny. Paulinyce apologized to the cops for her illegal and dumb bid to quench her thirst. Next time use the water fountain Paulinyce.......

A Plastic orgy, maybe? One wasn't enough! A 51 year old man was arrested in a Florida parking lot where he was engaged in a sexual romp with several blow-up sex dolls in the back seat of his car, in broad daylight. Stunned parents covered their kid's eyes until someone called police.

In the end he did not have a leg to stand on, ha, ha, ha. A paraplegic held up a Florida bank in his motorized wheelchair, and then stuffed the cash into his prosthetic leg. But he had not gotten far when police caught up with him ten minutes later.

Yeeeewww! Investigators say St. Lucie County firefighters who knew a paramedic took a man's severed foot from a vehicle crash site may face disciplinary action. Authorities said those who never reported the misconduct are being investigated. Cindy Economon resigned after admitting she took the foot to train her cadaver dog to locate and follow the scent of decomposing human flesh. She told investigators she took the foot belonging to the crash victim September 19, 2008, and was storing it in her home freezer.

Professor Birdsong has heard of a Fiddler on the Roof but this is ridiculous! The AP reports that somewhere in Florida a grandmother was arrested for driving around a grocery store parking lot with her baby granddaughter on the roof of her car. In her defense granny said she was driving at a snail's pace and holding the child's leg, and would never endanger her grand baby. Why?

No T.P., can you blame the guy for going off? A customer at a Florida gas station walked into the bathroom and emerged minutes later shouting, "You don't have any toilet paper!" and began pummeling the station's owner. Police arrived on the scene and arrested the man. Police said, "The PO'd customer hit the owner with his fists and whatever else he could grab."

Hint: When stealing beer and going on the run...choose cans and not bottles, dummy. A man in a Deland Publix grocery store was observed putting bottles of beer in his waistband. When confronted, he ran from the store. He dropped one bottle, but held onto two others until he tripped over a curb and fell. The bottles broke and the man suffered a laceration so severe that he was taken to the hospital for surgery. When he gets out of surgery police plan to arrest him for retail theft.

Bet pot smoking was involved in this heist. It's called getting the "munchies." Snack attack! Palm Bay police were able to track down a pack of teenage thieves who burglarized a house by following the trail of Reese's Peanut Butter Cup wrappers they left behind. Police found the five teens at one of their houses, where they confessed to burglary. Dummies...

Chapter Three

Dummies from Abroad

We find dumb criminals all around the world. This chapter consists of some of my favorite stories about dumb criminals from abroad. Hence, Dummies From Abroad.

England: Yuck!

A splash and grab robber took off with $10,000 after drenching his victim as she left an English bank. The thief soaked the woman by throwing water over her as she walked out the door, then helped dry her off before snatching her bag. It is the latest in a string of bizarre thefts that have involved victims being pelleted with paint, peanut butter and dog feces as they leave banks.

England: ZOOM!

A teenage girl who grabbed a 72-year-old British pensioner's purse picked the wrong old lady. That's because the victim had been a high school champion sprinter. Jean Hirst of Mansfield, was fast out of the starting blocks and covered 200 feet in less than 15 seconds to catch the culprit. "Suddenly I felt 18 again," said Hirst. The wayward girl "probably thought I was an easy target, but she shouldn't have judged a book by its cover," the sprightly septuagenarian added.

Wales, UK: Smoking is not good for you anyway.

A painter, Gordon Williams is fuming after being fined $60 for smoking in his "workplace" – after he lit up in his van. The Welsh decorator was stopped by police after he lit a cigarette while driving. Williams said, "I was told that, because my van is my place of work, I had broken the smoking laws. It's not my place of work. I decorate house, not vans."

Austria: He didn't need a fire...he needed glasses!

A western Austria farmer, an old timer from Angerberg, set his house afire after mistaking his fridge for his nearby fireplace. Adolf Maier, 87, piled wood into the open refrigerator and lit it. "I thought it was cold when I lit the match," he said. "Now I know why."

Austria: Sieg hiel my butt! Indeed!

This just was not funny! An Austrian tram driver was fired after bidding farewell to passengers with the Nazi salute "Sieg hiel!" When the passengers booed him, he responded by saying, "Can't you take a joke?" The transit authority didn't see the humor, though and called the statement "unspeakable." Use of Nazi symbols in Austria is a crime,

Germany: Tidy whiteys or boxers? Inquiring minds want to know.

This robber got away by the seat of his pants, but not for long. A German thief who grabbed a cell phone from a cabdriver near Cologne lost his trousers when his victim grabbed hold and tore them off. The man was arrested as he tried to board a train in his underpants.

Germany: No! It was not armed robbery.

A man with no arms managed to steal a TV from a German store. He made off with the 24-inch set using clamps that had been attached to his body by an accomplice. "It's hard to believe that the sight of an armless man walking along with a TV clamped to his body did not get anyone's attention," a police officer remarked.

Germany: DUMKOPF!

For some, not knowing the answer to a crossword clue is a serious problem. So serious in this case that a German woman called police for the answer to 5 Down. While angry police charged Petra Hirsch with wasting police time, they did give her the answer so it was worth it. I was totally stumped," said Hirsch. "It was really bothering me."

Hungary: Old, dumb and criminal!

An 83-year old Hungarian woman whose rap sheet dates to the 1950's has been arrested for breaking into a house. Kosztor Sandorne known as "Flying Gizi," for her habit of fleeing crime scenes by taking commercial flights, claimed she was in the house to try to save money on rent. She's been convicted more than 20 times for other crimes.

Nigeria: Why lock him up? How dangerous can a 114 year old be any way?

He did not live a life of crime, but now he is trying to make up for that fact. A 114 year old man was arrested in Nigeria after narcotics agents in Ogun State found 6 1/2 tons of marijuana in his home. Sulaiman Adebayo claims he thought the 254 sacks of weed contained only rice. For an 114 year this might be a good defense!

Mexico: Ay, Mamacita! Arriba, Arriba…

A supposedly paraplegic Mexican woman who begged for change while being pushed in a wheelchair through Monterrey by her husband "miraculously" regained her ability to run after a security guard caught them trying to break into a store. The couple was later arrested when they returned to get the wheelchair. Dummies…

Saskatchewan, Canada: What would he be rehabbing from, chicken plucking?

A Canadian man ran a-fowl of the law when he hurled chickens at several stores. Yelling, "Chickens are murder," the 20-year-old tossed a live bird into cooked-chicken displays at a Saskatchewan convenience store. Minutes later, two more came flying through the back door of a bar. The culprit was referred to a rehab program.

Poland: Go ahead...say it. He lied like a rug! Har, har, har.....

A crook on the lam from police tried to hide from police by rolling up in a giant rug and propping himself against a balcony as police searched his apartment. He was nabbed when one officer noticed the carpet was trembling. Miroslaw Babrowski faces 12 years in jail for armed robbery.

Poland: Ingrate!

A young man in Warsaw tried to turn in his mother for psychological torture -- after she told him to clean up his room. Police said Lukasz Zapalowski, 22, called police to rat out his mother -- who had merely told him to take a bath once a week, clean up his room and try to help her with the rent. Police said they may book him for wasting their time. Indeed!

Serbia: El Stupido!

Trying financial times call for creative solutions. Here was a stupid one. A ski-mask-wearing bandit robbed a bank in Serbia but was caught when he returned 30 minutes later -- without the mask-- to pay off his overdraft with the money he stole. Sharp-eyed employees recognized him from the bright red sneakers he wore both times.

Germany: What! No Lucy in the Sky with Diamonds?

The owner of a candy shop in Berlin was arrested for selling psychedelic sweets. Police said they found 120 pieces of magic mushroom chocolate and countless cannabis lollipops.

Germany: Yep, buck naked.

This German likes his hikes au naturel. German janitor Thomas Kranig has been jailed for 10 days for taking strolls without his clothes on. Naked outdoor pursuits have gained a following since the German Society of Nudists joined the German Sports Association.

Germany: He could defend himself on the grounds of "adverse possession."

A German man, tossed out of his girlfriend's apartment, has been living out of a luggage locker at the Dusseldorf train station for the past 10 years. Now authorities are trying to remove him and have him prosecuted for breach of the peace.

Germany: Ouch! Ouch! Ouch!

A skinny dipper in Germany who had broken into a community pool after closing hours fled from police when they tried to arrest him. The man had a painful, prickly end to his night when he fled right into a hedge of nettles. Police had no problem finding him. "The cops just followed the sound of the screaming," said a police spokesman.

Romania: What chutzpah.

Police in a remote part of this country pulled over a speeding car. The driver claimed he was Robert De Niro, the American actor. The man handed police ID papers bearing the star's name. Turns out the driver was part of a forgery gang.

Auckland, New Zealand: Sometimes the worm turns…

A New Zealander who raped a woman in his car was arrested after he fell asleep and she drove him to a police station. Vipul Sharma, 22, was convicted in November, 2008, of abduction and rape for the attack which occurred in 2006 in an Auckland park. After the assault he fell asleep – and woke up only after the victim had driven to the city's central police station. Police Detective Simon Welsh said, "She showed a lot of bravery and common sense. I have nothing but respect for what she has endured."

Taiwan: ...should have been charged with lunacy!

In Taiwan, it is a crime to throw your money away -- if you do it from a taxi. A man tossed $41,000 onto the streets from a taxi in a crowded part of Taichung city, causing a traffic jam as people rushed to grab the cash. "He might have had a nervous condition, as his state of mind wasn't normal," said the arresting police officer. The suspect was to be charged with public endangerment.

Austria: Yak, yak, yakity yak....

A court in Klagenfurt, Austria, fined a 73 year old mom $478 for phoning her son frequently -- up to 49 times a day. "I just wanted to talk to him," she told authorities after her son complained about her constant calls.

Austria: He would have been better off if he had just 'fessed up

An Austrian man who blew a small fortune at a casino staged a phony robbery because he was too afraid to tell his wife he had lost their money gambling. Josef

Reiner ended up in the hospital with a broken nose, jaw and arm after beating himself with an iron bar.

China: Idiot!

A Chinese burglar who stole a DVD player was arrested when he went back a month later to steal the remote control. When he broke into the Chengdu home a second time the owner, who was watching TV, promptly called police.

Bosnia: Doesn't sound like overkill...more like no kill!

Think this may be overkill? A man in Bosnia tried to murder his nagging mother in law with an anti-tank missile. And when she survived, Miroslav Miljici tried to finish her off with a machine gun. Amazingly, she survived both attacks with barely a scratch. Miljici -- who got six years for attempted murder -- told the court he could no longer take her incessant nagging.

South Korea: They do say that prayer can sometime move mountains...why not resurrection?

A woman in South Korea was under investigation when it was discovered that she had lived with her husband's corpse for 15 months in the belief that prayer would bring him back to life. Police say the man's body was effectively mummified and did not smell. No criminal charges were lodged.

China: Didn't work...the police did not come down with "moon fever."

A Chinese thief was cornered in an alley by police, and mooned them. Although the officers were taken aback, it didn't stop them from arresting him. He later said he thought his pursuers would be embarrassed and cover their eyes allowing him to escape. Dummy!

Chapter Four

A Few Drunken Dummies

Most of us take a drink from time to time with no adverse consequences. However, too much alcohol makes some people do some really, really dumb things. Here are a few closing stories about how dumb some people become when under the influence. Hence, A Few Drunken Dummies.

Professor Birdsong would surmise that there was actually a whole lot of alcohol involved. Two dozing burglars were arrested after they were found sleeping – one in a stolen hammock, the other in a pile of pilfered pillows – after swiping some patio furniture from a Monroe, Washington department store. Police found the snoozing pair after following a trail of pillows about 200 feet from the store. A Monroe police spokeswoman said, "We believe alcohol was involved."

Of all the joints in the world why did she have to walk into his? A South Dakota woman driving drunk picked the wrong person to ask for directions. When she pulled over and knocked on the door of a nearby home, a sheriff's deputy answered. The deputy told the 37 year old woman she could not get back behind the wheel of her truck. A wrestling match ensued. She lost and was charged with DWI.

Talk about hung out to dry! DWI and DWP -- driving without pants. A woman in Wisconsin crashed into a ditch after her pickup truck -- with her pants hanging out the window to dry -- veered off a highway. Jessica Jackson 29, had been chatting on her cell phone when she wrecked her truck outside the town of Plover. Police said she blew more than double the limit on the breathalyzer.

That's what alcohol Will do...An alleged drunk in Terre Haute, IN, who wrecked his car tried to get himself out of trouble by walking two miles to a farmhouse and taking a tractor to use as a makeshift tow truck. Kevin Michael Whitesell, 31, lost control as he hauled both vehicles and landed in a creek before fleeing.

Sounds like their own little highway to heaven, doesn't it. Three men and three women at a Terre Haute, Indiana prison have been charged with sneaking through a hole in the ceiling to have sex with each other. Having found a security camera blind spot, the inmates would climb into the ceiling, drink homemade liquor, play cards and do the wild thing.

What a hell cat! She's lucky they did not also charge her with "felony flooding." Police in Hailey, ID, say a woman battered a security guard, took off her clothes, punched two officers and bit a deputy. Now, Lori Brutsche-Ely, 41, faces several charges. Hailey Police Chief Jeff Gunther stated that the woman was intoxicated Halloween night at the Chester Jakes Restaurant in the Mint Bar when she got out of control. The Idaho Mountain Express newspaper reported that once she got to the jail, Brutsche-Ely bit a deputy and also managed to set off a fire sprinkler, causing her jail cell to flood. She has been charged with four counts of battery, obstructing and resisting arrest and indecent exposure.

Tsk, tsk, too young to be a designated driver. In mid August a 35 year old Texas woman was arrested after she made her 12 year old daughter drive her to a bar outside Houston. Police spotted the obviously unlicensed girl driving erratically. She told police she had dropped off her mom who was afraid to drive drunk.

She should have been driving a bumper car! A 20 year old New Jersey woman who got behind the wheel while drunk, and then fled the scene after smashing her car into a utility pole, was caught by police who tracked her using personal papers left at the crash scene, police said. However, before she could be arrested for the smashup, the unidentified woman crashed into a stone wall about two miles from the original accident.

Yep, reeeeeal intoxicated, but he really needed to cut his lawn. Keith Walendowski of Milwaukee was so furious when his lawn mower would not start that he took a gun and shot it. Walendowski was charged with felony possession of an unlicensed rifle. In his defense he said, "It's my lawn mower and my yard, so I can shoot it if I want." A witness told police Walendowski was most definitely intoxicated. Yep, reeeeeal intoxicated!

Youch! A booze fueled argument in Iowa between two buddies turned ugly when Donroy Merrival bit off the nose of Matthew Osring. The flesh and cartilage were not recovered, and Osring thinks his dogs may have eaten it.

And probably not a moment too soon. A naked man was arrested in Kennewick, Washington for allegedly masturbating while chasing a garbage truck. John Foster says he chased the truck because he was upset that the driver had looked at him. Foster was charged with public drunkenness.

This is a record you would really not want to set. A Rhode Island driver was arrested by police and found to have a blood alcohol level of .491 – six times the legal limit – and the highest ever recorded in the state for someone not dead. Health officials say a .4 is considered "comatose" and a .5 is fatal. Police said "Our only assumption could be that the person has a serious alcohol problem."

Goodness, gracious, great balls of fire! Two boozed up practical jokers in the California town of San Luis Obispo decided to mess with their passed out drinking buddy by setting his crotch on fire. It was reported that the man suffered second degree burns to his testicles. Again, alcohol was involved.

HIC! A man who walked into a convenience store in Waterloo, Iowa acted suspiciously and kept his hand in his pocket. The clerks, who had been robbed before, figured he must be a robber and threw a bag of money at him. He just looked at it and walked out. He was later arrested for public intoxication.

Cherche La Femme, as the French would say. This one is not about robbery. This one is about a guy who had his beer and drank it, too. Dennis LeRoy Anderson was charged with DWI after crashing his motorized La-Z-boy lounger into a parked car as he motored away from his local bar in Duluth. Anderson, 62, who had had nine beers before hopping into the contraption, claimed he was driving fine until a woman jumped in front of him, knocking him off course.

Yep, a real dope! A dopey 21-year old Oregon man was arrested after calling 911 to report his stash of marijuana had been stolen. Calvin Hoover told dispatchers that someone had broken into his vehicle and stole $400 and nearly an ounce of marijuana. Arriving police arrested him for DWI.

Often the Lord protects little children, fools and teens high on mushrooms. Seems everything was in slow-mo. A naked Virginia teenager high on psychedelic mushrooms was hit by a train but was unhurt because it was only going 9 miles per hour. Police found the youth lying comfortably under the train, and he ran off before deputies could get to him. They caught up with him in the woods several hours later.

The crime matched the costume. A Colonie, NY man dressed as a Breathalyzer unit for Halloween was arrested in Albany County for DWI. Theodore Piel, 24, actually refused to take the Breathalyzer exam, but still faces DWI charges. Arresting officers noted Piel's glassy eyes and a strong odor of alcohol, officials said. Ironic, no…

Clarksville, TN: Police in Clarksville arrested a woman who kept calling 911 to complain that a man refused to marry her. Hee Orama, 34, made multiple calls to say the guy promised to get hitched and then chickened out. A week earlier, she kept calling 911 to report she could not find her car. Yes, she was intoxicated when calling.

Just proves alcohol and aviation fuel do not mix. Here is a guy who watched the movie Heavy Metal too often. A 20 year old man broke into a small airport near San Jose, and filled his car up with aviation fuel because he thought it would make the vehicle fly and take him to some awesome, rocking worlds. Instead, he just ended up in jail for theft and driving drunk.

Liquor can do that to people. Police arrested a 30 year old Burnsville man for firing arrows into the side of a neighbor's townhouse. The suspect was trying to impress a woman, after they had been drinking and became "extremely intoxicated," police said. The woman told the police her pal wanted to "play Rambo."

Yes, the answer is yes…he was drunk! This may or may not be what they mean by marking your territory, Torey Devaux, a Wisconsin man, sought revenge on his roommate who refused to have sex with him by urinating on her dog. Devaux then shoved the woman's sister into a wall and punched out a window.

The End

About the Author

Professor Birdsong received his J.D. from the Harvard Law School and his B.A. from Howard University. He teaches law in Orlando, Florida.

After graduation from law school he worked four years at the law firm of Baker Hostetler. He then entered into a varied and distinguished career in government service. He served as a diplomat with the U.S. State Department with various postings in Nigeria, Germany and the Bahamas.

Professor Birdsong later served as a federal prosecutor. After leaving government service, and before he began teaching, Professor Birdsong was in private law practice in Washington, D.C.

www.BirdsongsLaw.com
lbirdsong@barry.edu

Ordering Information

New books coming soon!

Dear Reader,

If you liked this book, I would greatly appreciate you writing me a review on Amazon or any other book site.

I look forward to sharing more funny stories with you in future books.

Thank you, I really appreciate your help.

Regards,

Professor Birdsong

Winghurst Publications
1969 S. Alafaya Trail / Suite 303
Orlando, FL 32828-8732
www.BirdsongsLaw.com
lbirdsong@barry.edu

Other books by Professor Birdsong:

- Professor Birdsong's 77 Dumbest Criminals Stories (Kindle & Paperback)
- Professor Birdsong's 147 Dumbest Criminal Stories: Florida (Kindle)
- Professor Birdsong's 157 Dumbest Criminal Stories (Kindle & Paperback)
- Professor Birdsong's Weird Criminal Law Stories (Kindle)
- Professor Birdsong's "365" Weird Criminal Law Stories for Every Day of the Year (Kindle)
- Professor Birdsong's Weird Criminal Law Stories, Volume 2: Stories From Around the States and Abroad (Kindle)
- Professor Birdsong's Weird Criminal Law Stories, Volume 3: Stories From New York City and the East Coast. (Kindle)
- Professor Birdsong's Weird Criminal Law Stories - Volume 4: Stories from the Midwest (Kindle)
- Professor Birdsong's Weird Criminal Law Stories, Volume 5: Stories from Way Out West (Kindle)
- Professor Birdsong's Weird Criminal Law Stories - Volume 6: Women in Trouble (Kindle)

- Professor Birdsong's Weird Criminal Law - Volume 6: Women in Trouble! (Paperback)

55751968R00043

Made in the USA
Lexington, KY
02 October 2016

The Complete Book of DREAM Interpretation

Robert Wayne Pelton

ARCO PUBLISHING, INC.
NEW YORK

to
Karen Barron,
a dream of a friend

Published by Arco Publishing, Inc.
215 Park Avenue South, New York, N.Y. 10003

Library of Congress Cataloging in Publication Data

Pelton, Robert W., 1934–
The complete book of dream interpretation.

1. Dreams. I. Title.
BF1091.P43 1983 154.6'3 83-11825
ISBN 0-668-05735-1

Printed in the United States of America

10 9 8 7 6 5 4 3 2 1

Contents

	Preface	v
Part I	**Background to Dream Interpretation**	1
1	Introduction	3
2	Interpretation of Dreams	21
Part II	**Terrestrial Dream Dictionary**	27
3	Trees . . . Vines . . . Shrubs . . . Fruits . . . Nuts . . .	29
4	Animals	34
5	Birds	41
6	Precious Stones and Jewelry	46
7	Flowers, Vegetables, Herbs, and Grains	50
8	Insects, Fish, and Reptiles	55
9	People	59
10	Clothing	67
11	The Body	72

12	Human Actions	78
13	Food and Drink	91
14	Illness and Medicines	96
15	Ships and Related Items	100
16	Buildings	104
17	Contents of Buildings	108
18	Miscellaneous	115
Part III	**Celestial Dream Dictionary**	131
19	The Astral Plane	133
20	Symbols of the Heavenly Bodies	138
Part IV	**The Elements . . . Earth . . . Seasons . . . .**	141
21	Air . . . Fire . . . Water . . . Months	143

Preface

They answered again and said, Let the King tell his servants the dream, and we will shew the interpretation of it.

Daniel, 2:7

This is a unique dream dictionary. It represents the very ancient and mysterious Far Eastern interpretations for the very first time in book form. Long-lost secrets on the value of the psychic warnings in various dreams are given. They were carefully gleaned from a variety of ancient manuscripts found at a secluded monastary located deep in the mountains of Tibet.

It has been most exciting and interesting to sift through and study the many rare Oriental records of dreams and their symbolic meanings. These highly intelligent Asiatic people tended to see much less horror than those in the West. Among these centuries-old dream interpretations are many newer ones which, in relatively recent times, formed an important part of the lives of those who now reside in the Far East. A total of over two thousand dream interpretations are included.

The Bible abounds with references to dreams. Abraham Lincoln once said, "It seems strange how much there is about dreams in the Bible. There are sixteen chapters in the Old Testament and four or five in the New in which dreams are mentioned, and there are many other passages throughout the Bible, which refer to visions. If we believe the Bible, we must accept the fact that many things are made known in our dreams."

Many authorities believe there is no longer any doubt that the future *is* revealed through the strange world of dreams. Dreaming is and always has been a universal phenomenon. For thousands of years, man has toyed with attempts at accurate dream interpretation. There was a time in history when all dreams were believed to be Divine messages and professional seers were handsomely rewarded for producing feasible explanations.

An interesting example is that of Xerxes, who had given in to the arguments of Artabanus and decided to stop fighting in the war with Greece. While sleeping one night, Xerxes was visited in a dream by a handsome man. The ghost-like figure said to the king: "You renounce your purpose of waging war against the Greeks after placing your armies in the field? Know, then, that if you do not resume the expedition, in a short time you will be as lowly as today you are proud and haughty!"

The dream was repeated for three consecutive evenings. The astonished monarch called for Artabanus, and, after telling him about his dream, commanded him to attire himself in royal clothing. Artabanus was forced to sleep in the king's massive bed, in order to determine whether or not Xerxes had been duped by an illusion.

Artabanus complied with Xerxes' wishes for he didn't want to offend the king. He had scarcely fallen asleep when the same apparition appeared to him in a dream. The young man said: "Artabanus, I have already declared to the king what will happen to him should my orders be disobeyed. Cease thyself to oppose the decrees of fate!"

The phantom's eyes sparked with anger as he bellowed out his orders. Artabanus was terrified and frantically leaped up out of bed. He ran to see Xerxes and explained what had transpired. Xerxes considered the dream to be an omen of certain victory for his Persian armies, so he again started battling the Greeks. But it was too late, for the king had hesitated in obeying the orders of the apparition. The war's disastrous ending made good the prophecy of the dream, and Xerxes was soon "as lowly as today you are proud and haughty."

Such dreams of a prophetic nature occurred in many instances in the early history of the world, and the courts of numerous

Oriental princes were attended by learned seers, whose only task was to correctly interpret dreams. In the most ancient civilized cultures of which there is a record—those of Babylon and Egypt—to interpret a monarch's dream was one of the most important state offices. Grave philosophers wrote entire treatises on the interpretation of dreams, as well as on astrology and other occult sciences.

No one really knows why we dream, yet it is an accepted fact that in sleep we see without being awakened—for we witness the angry lightning shoot through the mighty clouds, and we hear the explosive thunder hurl its fury at us. Why this is so, no one can yet explain satisfactorily. Many strange and wonderful revelations have come to us through a dream. Marriage, divorce, a broken engagement, financial losses, sickness, and even death have been foretold with remarkable accuracy through the interpretation of a dream. Many inventions as well as fortunes have had their beginning in a dream. How often we hear of a poem, a play, a song, a piece of music, or even an entire book that was founded on the mere fabric of a dream.

There certainly is important information to be gained from the point of view of psychology and psychic influence, for those far-sighted individuals who wish to interpret dreams for other than simply a passing amusement. Oriental seers and astrologers of antiquity classed all dreams according to their symbolism in specific groupings. These long-forgotten interpretations are presented herein in exactly that same manner.

ILLUSTRATED

DREAM BOOK

INCLUDING

MYSTIC KNOWLEDGE

Published by

WEHMAN BROS.

A popular book published in 1891.

PART I

BACKGROUND TO DREAM INTERPRETATION

CHAPTER 1

Introduction

A dream which is not understood is like a letter which is not opened.

Talmud

Dreams and the need to uncover their hidden meanings are as ancient as humanity. This desire to discern the unknown is even found among the most primitive peoples on earth. Dream interpretation is interwoven with native religion, a powerful force that is heavily blended with witchcraft and occultism.

Dreams have always been highly regarded in every society. Such is revealed by early writings. Positions of authority were held by prophets and diviners of dreams. Their influence was unmatched in all state business and in the area of religion. The continuing study and recording of dream data by notable scholars in all historical eras indicate that the interest in the value of dream interpretation will never cease.

The Bible is filled with a multitude of excellent dream data—both in the Old and the New Testaments. Throughout the entire Bible there is abundant evidence of a belief in the supernatural origin of dreams. It was an accepted and honored means of communication between the Deity and his chosen ones, for it is written: "I will pour out my Spirit upon all flesh; and your sons and daughters shall prophesy, your old men shall dream dreams, and your young men shall see visions."

The best-known dreams of the Old Testament are those of Daniel, Jacob, and Joseph. Some authorities claim that the Book of Daniel was written from a dream. The Book of Daniel contains a number of prophetic dreams which were fulfilled to the letter. The insanity of Nebuchadnezzar and his downfall were presaged. So was the eventual overthrow of the despotic Belshazzar.

Daniel

Jacob was a man who had many dreams. His dream of the celestial ladder uniting heaven and earth constitutes one of the most beautiful passages in Genesis. His father-in-law, Laban, was warned in a dream that he must not harm Jacob. In another instance, a distressed King Saul cries out, "God is departed from me, and answereth me no more, neither by prophets, nor by dreams."

Joseph, the son of Jacob, was widely known as the "dreamer."

While he was in Egypt and working for the pharaoh, the Egyptian monarch had the famous prophetic dream of the fat and lean cattle. Joseph interpreted this dream as a warning of a coming famine. He said: "God hath shewed pharaoh what he is about to do." This dream is credited with saving Egypt from famine and Joseph was aptly rewarded by being appointed chief advisor to the king. The birth of Jesus Christ was also foretold to Joseph in one of his many dreams.

Dreams play a major role as warnings throughout the New Testament. The Holy Family was advised in a dream to go into Egypt. Pontius Pilate's wife warned him after she had a vivid dream at the time of the crucifixion: "Have thou nothing to do with that just man: for I have suffered many things this day in a dream because of him!"

Paul was a man who dreamed with regularity. Many of the apostles were initially converted to Christianity after experiencing dreams. A multitude of subsequent saints were strongly influenced by dreams—among them is St. Augustine.

Egyptian priests of days gone by were highly skilled in this field. So were the most notable scholars of Greece. The *Delphic Oracle of Delos* was held in great esteem. It was so revered that learned people would never seriously consider taking a trip, initiating any new business, or entering into a marriage without first carefully consulting the oracle.

Rome's most educated citizens, as well as those of Athens, devoted much time to contemplating and then writing about dreams. These included such notables as Socrates and Plato. Plato contended that there were divine manifestations to the soul during sleep. Dreams are ascribed a supernatural origin by Homer, and in the Greek and Roman classics are numerous descriptions of unusual prophetic dreams.

Aristotle wrote a major treatise on dream interpretation, as did Astrampsychus. Says Aristotle: "There is a divination concerning some things in dreams not incredible." Synesius placed dreaming above all other methods of divining the future. He believed it was the most accurate, and liked the method because it was always open to the poor and the rich alike.

Artemdorus Dalidarius alone took it upon himself to compile

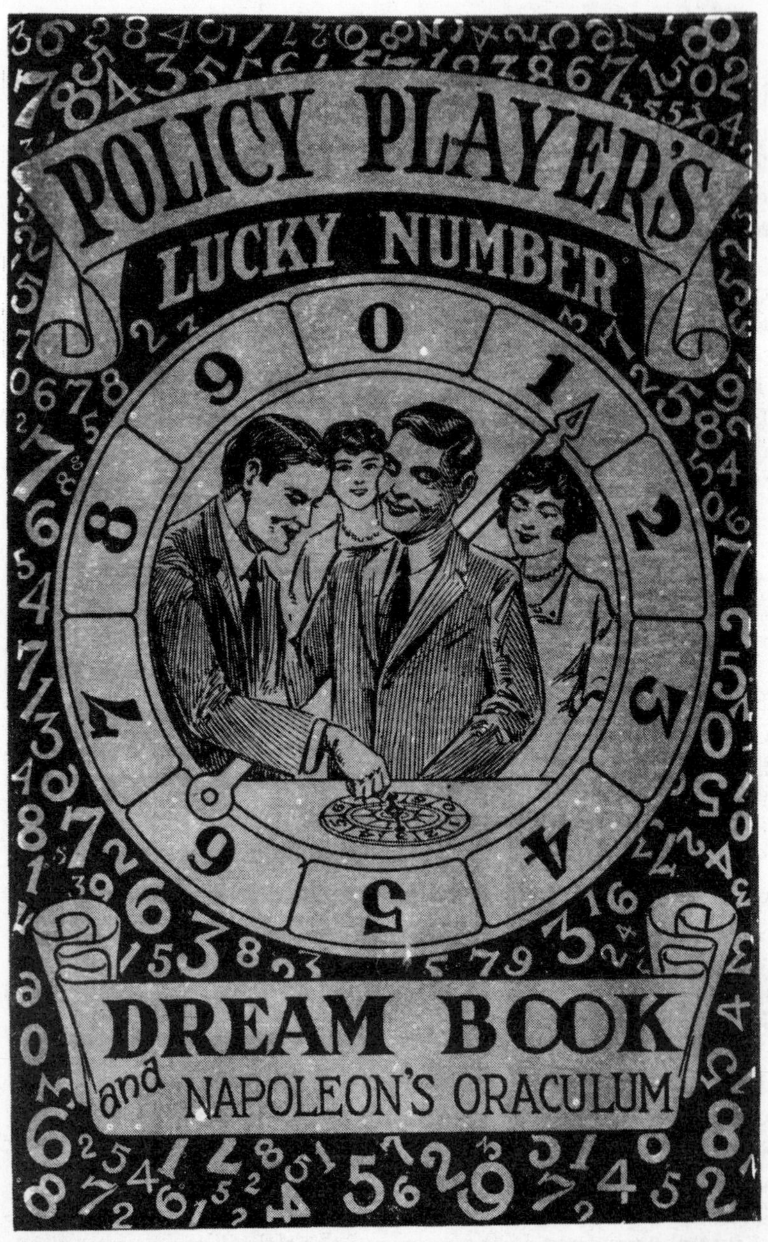

One of the most successful dream books as it appeared in paperback.

An extremely popular dream book from the late 1800s.

Socrates

Plato

Homer

Aristotle

five volumes on the subject of dreams. His was probably the earliest published material on the subject. It was translated and printed in book form in seventeenth century London. During the Marsic War (90 B.C.), the Roman senate ordered that the temple honoring Juno Sospita be rebuilt. This was the end result of a dream by Caecilia Metalla, wife of Roman consul Appius Claudius Pulcher.

Many kings and queens have been given warnings of impending danger through a dream. Caesar, on the night before he was murdered, continually had the same dream. He saw himself "soaring above the clouds on wings." And he saw himself placing his "hand within the right hand of Jove." Caesar's wife also tried to warn him on the impending danger. She, too, had experienced a terrible dream the evening prior to his assassination. Shakespeare tells us:

Julius Caesar

Thrice hath Calpurnia in her sleep cried out,
"Help, ho! they murder Caesar!"

Cassius of Parma, a supporter of Mark Anthony in a political power struggle, fled Rome and hid in Athens after the difficult battle of Actium. He was sleeping one night and dreamed of a tall, heavy-set, dark man who snarled: "I am your evil genius." The ghastly apparition appeared again and again in his dreams, always saying exactly the same thing. Cassius was frightened, but never fully realized the warning he was being given. Early the next morning, he was brutally murdered by order of Emperor Augustus.

Chrysippus wrote a treatise on dreams and said that he considered them to be divine portents. He refers to the skilled interpretation of dreams as an accurate means of divination, but notes that, like all other arts in which man has to proceed on conjecture, it is far from infallible.

Cicero writes of two traveling Acardians who visited the city of Megara. One went to stay with friends, the other got a room at a local inn. The man who lodged with his friends had a shattering dream that his traveling companion was calling out to him for assistance. The innkeeper was going to kill the man. The dreamer awoke in a sweat, brushed off the horrible dream as nonsense, and proceeded to go back to sleep. His friend at the inn appeared in still another dream, this time to tell him it was now too late. He said he had already been murdered, his body tossed in a wooden cart, and covered with dung. Lastly, he revealed that his murderer would try to sneak his body out of town the very next morning. The dreamer now quickly got up, went to see the local authorities, and had the cart searched. The dead body of his friend was easily located and the killer was brought to justice.

The Emperor Marcian dreamed that he saw the bow of the Hunnish conqueror break. This took place on the same night Attila met his death. Plutarch reveals how Augustus, while sick, was persuaded he should leave his tent after being told of a dream's prophetic warning by a close friend. A few short hours

Mark Anthony

Cicero

Augustus

later, his enemies moved in and the bed on which Augustus had slept was pierced by many swords. Heeding a friend's dream saved this leader's life.

Croesus witnessed his son being killed in a dream. And Petrarch clearly talked to his beloved Laura in a dream on the day she died. This dream was the inspiration for his lovely poem, "The Triumph of Death." And even Joan of Arc presaged her own death in one of her dreams.

Petrarch

Goethe declares frankly in his memoirs, "The objects which had occupied my attention during the day often reappeared at night in connected dreams. On awakening, a new composition, or a portion of one I had already begun, presented itself to my mind."

The distinguished violinist, Tartini, composed the "Devil's Sonata" after having a most unusual dream. According to Tar-

Goethe

tini, Satan appeared in his dream and challenged him to a contest of playing skills. When he awoke, the music played by the Devil was burned into his mind. He easily committed the entire composition to paper.

John Bunyan, author of the classic *Pilgrim's Progress,* attributed this piece of literature to an inspiration given him in his dreams. Coleridge, the poet, once fell asleep in his chair while reading a book. He had just taken some opium as medication for an illness. He slept soundly for three hours. Upon awaken-

Samuel T. Coleridge

ing, the man had an indelible impression in his mind for a poem. He immediately wrote the immortal lines of *Kubla Khan*.

Cabanis, the widely respected philosopher, always solved his most insurmountable problems by dreaming. Benjamin Franklin seldom worried while awake and working. He dreamed often while asleep and found this to be a marvelous way to get correct answers to seemingly unsolvable situations.

President Abraham Lincoln and his wife were spending part of a quiet afternoon visiting with friends in the White House. It was Good Friday, April 14, 1865. He described a haunting dream he had recently experienced.

> **About ten days ago I retired very late . . . I soon began to dream. There seemed to be a deathlike stillness about me. Then I heard subdued sobs as if a number of people were weeping. I thought I had left my bed and wandered downstairs.**
>
> **There the silence was broken by the same pitiful sobbing, but the mourners were invisible. I went from room to room.**

Benjamin Franklin

No living person was in sight, but the same mournful sounds of distress met me as I passed along. Every object was familiar to me, but nowhere could I see the people who were grieving as though their hearts would break. I was puzzled and alarmed. Determined to find the cause of a state of things so mysterious and so shocking, I kept on until I arrived at the East Room. There I met with a sickening surprise. Before me was a catafalque, on which rested a corpse wrapped in funeral vestments. Around it were stationed soldiers who were acting as guards; and there was a throng of

Abraham Lincoln

people, some gazing mournfully at the corpse, whose face was covered, others weeping pitifully.

"Who is dead in the White House?" I demanded of one of the soldiers. "The President," was his answer. "He was killed by an assassin." Then came a loud burst of grief from the crowd, which awoke me from my dream. It is only a dream but it has strangely annoyed me, however. Let us say no more about it.

Dreams are not always as crystal clear with their warnings as was the Lincoln dream. They are quite often only symbolic. Therefore, a good dream book has immense value in assisting the dreamer in interpreting and then properly utilizing the con-

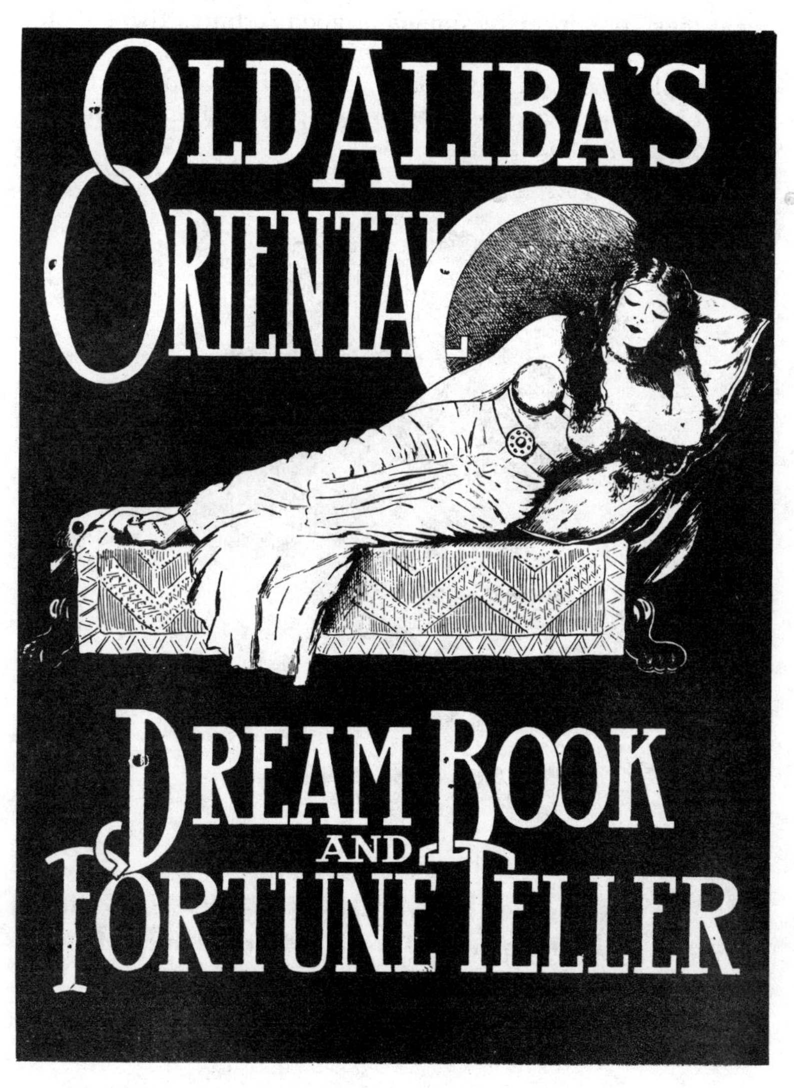

A rare edition of a dream book published in the early 1900s.

tents of his or her dreams. A dream appearing to be insignificant may contain many omens of good fortune. These should inspire the dreamer to try something new or to push ahead with former plans. Any dire warnings, if considered seriously, could turn out to be invaluable—as proper preparation may help to win out in the final analysis.

William Shakespeare

Let the final thought be that of Shakespeare:

> **If I may trust the flattering eye of sleep,**
> **My dreams presage some joyful news at hand.**

CHAPTER 2

Interpretation of Dreams

Then thou scarest me with dreams, and terrifiest me through visions.

Job, 7:14

There is much interest and loads of fun in store when attempting to properly interpret a dream either for ourselves or for friends and acquaintances. Any individual can readily become very skillful in the interpreting and combining of the dream symbols and the surrounding conditions. First decide on the category of the particular dream (terrestrial, celestial, or the elements). Then turn to the Dream Dictionary, Part II, Part III, or Part IV for the meanings of the most important symbols. If there are several different symbols in any one of the lists, carefully scan the preface explanation of each chapter before trying to interpret the dream.

Says Camille Flammarion, the great French astronomer, in *Premonitory Dreams and Divination of the Future*: "I do not hesitate to affirm at the outset that occurrence of dreams foretelling future events with accuracy must be accepted as certain."

Human activities, attire, food, and illness will be easily found categorized under Part II. This section is divided into special classifications with important notes preceding each grouping. Physical actions seen in a dream are of great importance. Read these words handed down by Herodotus: "Hippias led the barbarians to Marathon after he had the following dream-vision the previous night. It had seemed to Hippias that he was sleeping with his own mother. He concluded from this dream that he would return home to Athens, and would regain power, and that he would die in his fatherland in his old age."

The numerous sensations felt by the dreamer when they accompany the various symbols should be carefully recorded. These include such things as danger, sensuality, nervousness, fear, pleasure, discomfort. Any sounds or noises heard in a dream have a unique psychic meaning. The same is true of any words the dreamer reads, hears, or speaks.

Andre Pujor was on his way to Paris and stopped over in Riom. He got a room at the local inn and went to sleep for the night. He dreamed that the anagram of his name was *pedu a Riom* (hung at Riom). In the morning, he and the innkeeper had an argument over the bill, and Andre killed the man in a fit of anger. Eight days later, Andre Pujor was executed by hanging—thus the presage of the unusual dream was verified.

In Part II, Chapter 18, under *Miscellaneous,* many things will be found that are not specifically covered in any other classes. Among these are colors, musical instruments, and numbers; all of which have great psychic importance. Numbers may refer to an important time, or to impending events, a special day, or even the correct series of numbers required to win at the races, or in a lottery. When a number is very clear, it may indicate an extremely important date.

Mabel Barnes of Brooklyn, New York, made a habit of promising her niece substantial wealth, but the poor old lady was never able to fulfill her promise before she finally died. Shortly after her death, Mabel appeared in a phantom-like state during a dream the young niece was having. She was seen drawing a series of numbers on a wall. She reappeared and again inscribed the identical numbers, while whispering the word, "lottery." The niece went out the next day and purchased a lottery ticket. The one handed to her bore the same numbers that had been

A very popular book on dreams made its appearance during the early 1900s.

given to her in the previous night's dream. She subsequently won handsomely.

Dreams of the celestial bodies divulge many remarkable incidents as well as an ascension to fame and fortune. They are thoroughly covered in Part III, Chapters 19 and 20. Atmospheric conditions—sunshine, rain, storms, and so forth—should be initially deliberated followed by physical activities. Next to be considered are the sensations felt by the dreamer—especially the most vivid feelings. Lastly, the various symbols are acknowledged in the order of distinctiveness of impression made on the dreamer. Sunshine is always taken to be a marvelous omen, unless it is so scorching as to be uncomfortable, or unless it is causing other things to burn. All of this and more is carefully covered under *The Elements,* in Part IV.

If many different objects appear in a particular dream, the prevailing aspect of them, aside from the state of the weather or physical feelings, is interpreted. The most outstanding items are to be initially examined. Nothing in the dream should be omitted, even when it may seem to be relatively minor. Even an insignificant person or thing may be the solution to what at first appears confusing or contradictory.

The major items may tend to all be equally as strong in a dream. First analyze all the favorable symbols. Then analyze the unfavorable omens. If the positive signs outweigh the negative signs, it denotes that all obstacles or problems can and will be overcome. But, if there is a majority of foreboding signs, the time is not right to initiate any kind of new ventures, seek a job, locate a new lover, or rush into any new undertaking. Success is not possible for there will be too many things in the way.

Some dreams are interpreted in reverse. Among these are weak feelings of apprehension, disappointment, or even sadness and anger. This is often the case when the major symbols are highly favorable. For example, when a poor person dreams of losing everything, it's a good sign for it indicates a turn away from misfortune. If a wealthy individual has this identical dream, it then bears its true significance. This same principle applies to anyone who is ill. If a sick person dreams of illness, it usually represents the opposite—good health is on the way. But, should a healthy person have such a dream, he can be almost certain that illness is fast approaching.

When one dreams of cultivated fruit, vegetables, or flowers, any unfavorable omen is canceled if they appear during the wrong season. There are a few exceptions to this rule.

When interpreting a dream for a friend or a relative, always try to make complete sentences from the material covered under each category. Use the explanations given as a basic guide for your findings. And finally, ponder the words of Lynkeus: "Your marvelous faculty of dreaming as if you were awake is based upon your virtue, upon your goodness, your justice, and your love of truth; it is the moral charity of your nature which makes everything about you intelligible."

PART II

TERRESTRIAL DREAM DICTIONARY

CHAPTER 3

Trees . . . Vines . . . Shrubs . . . Fruits . . . Nuts . . . .

Dreams, according to Freud, are the royal road to the unconscious. . . . Unfortunately, it is a road that is easily lost if there is not full knowledge of all the territory around it.

Karen Horney

Anything in this category that grows fast and stays healthy is an excellent omen. The more luxurious a plant appears to the dreamer, the better the good fortune. A vine that bears no fruit, when seen strangling a tree or other plant, is always taken as a dire warning. The dreamer must ever be alert to offset danger and evil.

When a dream concerns a tree being chopped or sawed down, it is a prediction of success unless the particular tree happens to carry an unfavorable connotation. Cutting down a tree presaging something good indicates misfortune for the dreamer. Problems will arise because of stupid activities, bad decisions, and so forth. But when the felled tree is a bad omen to begin with, a change of luck for the better will quickly take place. If you dream of falling out of a tree, it is a sign warning of losing a job, monetary losses, or a decrease in social standing in the community.

"Dreams so often seem to be without meaning, or even nonsensical," suggests Lynkus. "But in the profoundest sense, this is by no means the case; indeed it cannot be."

A fertile, well-kept orchard is a fortunate sign. If the trees are blossoming, great luck is in store for lovers; and families will experience more stability and bliss. If the trees in the orchard are bearing ripe apples, pears, plums, and so on, it represents a gain in every area of life. If the fruit is green, new opportunities are available for the dreamer. If the apples are small and scarce, success will be less than expected. Lots of healthy green leaves will make up for any lack of fruit.

Finding yourself in the woods presages a great deal of money for those who do not believe that they are lost. Becoming lost in the woods denotes an abundance of unexpected obstacles in the way of success. Hard times can be expected if the woods appear to have been recently burned. The same is true if all the trees lack leaves. If the dream shows only tree stumps in the woods, failure in all endeavors can be expected.

An interesting example of a dream regarding vines is one in which Astyages, King of the Medes, dreamed that his lovely daughter had given birth to a vine. This was a prediction of the greatness, happiness, and wealth of Cyrus, his daughter's child, born shortly after he had the dream.

Acorns: Excellent prospects in everything attempted
Almond: Contentment and harmony throughout life
Apple: Joy and amusement will soon come

Apple (sour): Many quarrels and arguments. Possible heartbreak
Apricot: Peace of mind and many pleasures in store
Arbor: A love affair is close
Arbor (inside): Many obstacles to happiness in love
Ash: Affection may result in love
Aspen: Foolish fears prevent success in accomplishments
Banana: Plenty of everything in life—contentment
Barberry: Good cheer in spite of troubles
Bay: Protection against evil things and illness
Bay (withered): A certain sign of death
Blossoms: Good fortune in love affairs
Blossoms (budding): New happiness and pleasures soon coming
Blossoms (withered or blighted): Disappointment in love matters
Brambles or briars: Many difficulties to overcome
Brambles or briars (hurting): Loss of influential friends
Burrs: Intriques and entanglements
Butternut: Hardships will be followed by good things
Cedar: Unlimited successes in every endeavor
Cherry: A good time with many close friends
Chestnut: Love and kindness will lighten your sorrow
Coconut: Plans are endangered by an unknown enemy
Christmas tree: Good fortune and joyful events
Christmas tree (without ornaments): Disappointment at festivities
Christmas tree (discarded): Loss of prestige or esteem
Currants: Successful enterprises, happiness, and faithful love
Cypress: Affliction and much sadness
Date: Everything will be most plentiful
Ebony: The task will be difficult but worthwhile pursuing
Elderberry: Social rise, wealth, happiness, and contentment
Elm: Many honors and great dignity will envelop your life
Evergreen: Wonderful prosperity for everyone around you; *also see* Christmas tree
Fig: Much pleasure and a life full of joy

Fig (withered): Great distress in life to soon come
Filbert: Reconciliation with lovers and friends
Gooseberry: Keen rivalry in love affairs
Grapes: Happiness, joy, and great profit to come
Grapefruit: Happiness will be marred by jealousy
Hazel: Many new friends and pleasant companionship
Hawthorne: Secret love meetings
Hedge: Protection from intruders is around you
Hedge (if caught in): Many serious obstacles to conquer
Ivy: Many faithful lovers and close friends
Laurel: Ultimate victory over obstacles and great honors
Lemon: Envy will cause unexpected troubles
Lemon (moldy): Marriage separation or love split-up
Lemon (eating): Great humiliation
Limes: Serious illness or injury
Locust: Love and contentment at home
Mulberry: Hard work will eventually bring peace of mind
Mulberry (eating berries): Vexation and much sadness
Mulberry (overly ripe): A speedy marriage for lovers
Nectarine: Something unusual is about to happen unexpectedly
Nuts: An abundance of everything
Nuts (hard to open): Success only to come through hard work
Nuts (eating): Exciting and worthwhile experiences
Oak: Long life, honors, and riches
Olive: Peace of mind and enjoyment in life
Orange: Good health and a favorable future
Orange (blossoms): A wedding in the near future
Orange (eating): Bitter disappointments can be expected
Orange (spotted or withered): Unhappiness in marriage
Palm: Great happiness for all. Bliss in marriage
Pear: Serenity and happy times
Pecan: Failure will soon turn to success
Persimmon: An unusual, unpleasant experience
Pine: Success with hard work
Pineapple: Good fortune in all things
Plums: Life will be fun and full of laughter
Poison ivy: Good friends will deceive. They are really enemies
Pomegranate: Will make new and very influential friendships

Poplar: A favorable sign in every way
Prunes: Good health and much happiness
Quince: Good clean fun with friends
Raspberries: Pleasures are doubtful
Roots: Prosperity is not immediately forthcoming
Roots (medicinal): Health will be restored after an illness
Shrubs (green): Success in all small undertakings
Shrubs (leafless): Trifling disappointments
Shrubs (withered): A series of insignificant failures
Strawberries: Extremely good fortune, especially for lovers
Strawberries (wild): Unexpected good luck is soon forthcoming
Sycamore: Sorrow caused by jealousy in marriage
Thicket: Persistency will overcome difficulties
Thorns: Spite and envy will create difficulties
Tulip tree: Wonderful times to come, especially for lovers
Vines: Abundance of everything and happiness
Vines (blossoming): Marital bliss and happy love
Vines (destroying): Entanglements to try and avoid
Vines (fruitful): Increasing riches and family size
Walnut: Kindness will bring happiness
Willow: Loving friends will help console through sadness
Willow (weeping): Loved one will forsake you
Witch hazel: Good health and contentment; recovery for the ill
Woodbine: Warm and faithful friends will assist
Wood pile (meager or disorderly): Idleness will bring bad luck
Wood pile (plentiful and orderly): Security in all financial areas
Yew tree: Disappointment and sickness
Yew tree (dead): An inheritance is on the way

CHAPTER 4

Animals

And Joseph dreamed a dream, and he told it his brethren; and they hated him yet the more.

Genesis, 37:5

Just before the famous battle of Waterloo, Napoleon dreamed that two black cats were running back and forth between the opposing armies. One of the cats, his, was finally shredded to ribbons. Napoleon, aware of the deadly omen, suffered a humiliating disaster and lost the battle the very next day.

If a dream concerns an animal who appears to be fat and healthy, it adds much force to the meaning of that particular omen. By the same token, a lean or sickly animal represents a lessening of the influence. When an animal is seen to be starving or in poor health, and this can be changed through better care and feeding, it shows that the adverse sign can be subdued through understanding and effort.

When the fur or hair is luxurious and thick, then this too adds to the strength of the dream. Healthy herds of cattle or flocks of sheep denote good fortune in business matters. If the dream relates to the feeding of these animals, it indicates that the

Napoleon

dreamer's work will be highly rewarded. Seeing cattle or other farm animals go into a pool of water (pond, lake, river) is far from a favorable sign. If they refuse to drink any of the water, or if the animals muddy the water, the omen is even worse.

Any wild or ferocious beasts denote impending danger from prominent or influential people. If the dreamer is wounded or even attacked by an animal, danger and problems will befall him or her causing serious mishaps or illnesses.

General farm animals are always a choice sign for marriage. Manure signifies great wealth. Contented pigs and hogs seen in a relatively clean pigsty are also a sign of an increase in riches.

Dirty living quarters with starving pigs denotes sadness and dishonor through greed.

Dreaming of riding a healthy animal predicts help from powerful sources to be near at hand. But if the dreamer falls from the animal, or if thrown, it represents debasement and demeaning conduct.

A dream concerning trapping animals, or even seeing one of them in a snare, is a serious warning of danger through self-indulgence and avarice.

If an animal comes to the dreamer to be petted, it represents that friends are available who truly care. When an animal denoting a bad omen seems to be friendly in a dream, then expect to be deceived and taken advantage of in the very near future. Other evil influences may also be forthcoming.

An interesting story can be found in the annals of Valerius Maximus, regarding a dream that took place while the Romans were involved in the Macedonian war. Publius Vatinius was sleeping in Rome when he saw two young men suddenly come before him in a dream. Both were riding beautiful white horses. The handsomest of the two made a proclamation to the sleeping Publius that Perseus, the king of Macedon, had been taken prisoner the day before by the Roman consul, Paulus Emilius.

Vatinius woke with a start and found it was early morning. He dressed and hastened over to the senate in an effort to share the joyous tidings. But the senators, refusing to believe the man, ordered him cast into prison. In the course of time, official word finally came from consul Emilius, verifying that the king of Macedon had indeed been captured on the day cited previously by Vatinius. The senate immediately had the prisoner released from prison, apologized publicly, and gave him a gift of land. It was also ordained that henceforth Castor and Pollux were to be regarded as patrons of the great Roman Empire.

To dream of an elephant signifies, according to Artemidorius, fear and peril. But according to Apomazor, the Arabian seer, it denotes a wealthy person. His logic: if a man dreams he is carried on an elephant's back, he surely will be given gifts of great value and he will be granted the favor of some great world leader.

On the other hand, Artemidorius tells of having known a rich woman in Italy who dreamed regularly of riding an elephant. The dream portended serious illness. And he also says that if anyone is to dream of feeding an elephant, that person is fated to join destinies with someone who is on the way up to fame and fortune.

The Queen Olympia was pregnant with Alexander the Great when she experienced an unusual dream. She saw her husband, Philip, give her a seal which was engraved with the picture of a lion. This dream, when interpreted, presaged the fame and subsequent conquests of her illustrious son.

Ape: Sickness and distress expected soon
Ass: A quarrelsome but faithful friend will turn on you
Badger: An unpleasant enemy comes into your life
Bat: Strange and unfortunate news in immediate future
Bear: Attack by a powerful enemy will come unexpectedly
Bear (killing): Escape from an entanglement is foretold
Beaver: Hard work will bring enough for comfort only
Boar: A savage and pitiless foe is seen attacking
Buffalo: A huge undertaking will be successful and profitable
Bull: An influential person will offer aid
Bull (attacked by): Opposition and oppression foreseen soon
Calf: Speedy good fortune can be expected
Calf (many): Assured success in all endeavors
Camel: Wealth but not always happiness for the dreamer
Camel (riding on): Rough road to success for a short time
Cat (black): Good luck with all things in life
Cat (black), TWO OF THEM: Disaster
Cat (scratched by): Sickness due soon
Cat (spitting or quarreling): Slander by false friends expected
Cat (strange): A subtle thief to take advantage
Cat (white): A faithful friend offers assistance
Cat (wild): A fierce opponent will try to harm
Cow: Wealth obtained through honesty
Cow (being milked): Good fortune in the near future for friends
Deer: True friendship and a happy marriage to come
Deer (hunting): Failure through sensual pleasures
Deer (killing): Failure and much sorrow
Dog: Fidelity and devotion from lover

Dog (bitten by): Troubles through unjust accusation and envy
Dog (dirty): Illness
Dog (lean): Distress in business matters
Dog (strange): A dangerous enemy to enter the picture
Dolphin: A change of position, or in those supervising you
Donkey: Hard work will bring moderate success
Donkey (braying): Humiliation in public by a friend
Dromedary: Affluence and honors. A favorable sign for lovers
Elephant: Influence used in your favor for new job
Elephant (riding one): Success spoiled by illness
Elk: Loss of property and danger to life soon to come
Elk (many): Forced abandonment of a project you love
Ermine: A cunning enemy appearing as a friend to hurt you
Ferret: An unscrupulous person who seeks to ruin you
Fox: Quarrels with a shrewd adversary. May result in problems
Fox (tame): One of the opposite sex creates scandal
Goat (black): Opposition and bad luck
Goat (white): Excellent luck in everything
Hare: Opportunity to engage in new enterprises
Hare (crossing path): Success delayed for a week
Hog: Improvement and changes in business and love life
Hog (squealing): Unpleasant news strikes unexpectedly
Horse (bay): Rise in fortune and success in love matters
Horse (black): Wealth by dubious methods and infidelity
Horse (dead): Disappointment unless the horse is black
Horse (killing): Loss of friends through selfishness and jealousy
Horse (riding): On the road to success and possible fame
Horse (running away): Beware of rash actions under pressure
Horse (white): Prosperity and pleasure in all areas of life
Horseshoe: Good luck in everything
Horseshoe (broken): Illness and temporary bad luck unavoidable
Horseshoe (finding): Great good luck for dreamer and friends
Hyena: An evil and dangerous associate will cause problems
Kangaroo: Something most extraordinary to surprise you
Kids: Consolation after bereavement by unexpected sources
Lamb: Peace amid harmonious surroundings forthcoming
Leopard: Varying fortune, now up, then down; be patient

Lion: Friendship with distinguished people to come
Lion (fighting): Struggle against strong opposition to be expected
Lion (riding one): Influential assistance will be offered
Lion (victory over): Successful outcome of important matters in love
Lynx: Sly enemies in business, untrustworthy relatives, an unscrupulous rival for lovers
Mare: Kindness and contentment generally in life
Mare (catching): Success in love and marriage
Mare (to saddle): Early marriage foreseen within months
Menagerie: Limitation of activities unless animals are caged; if so, it denotes safety in all endeavors
Mole: An enemy who works secretly against you
Monkeys: Mischievous friends and vexatious enemies to be expected
Monkeys (many): Múch irritation and many problems
Mouse: Extravagance nibbles away good fortune; enemies in sight
Mules: Stubborn but steadfast friend will hurt feelings
Mules (many): Difficulties to overcome with persistence
Otter: Happiness in love and marriage guaranteed
Oxen: A faithful friend or employee will come to aid
Oxen (many): A year of plenty unless they are lean, then it means famine
Panther: A fashionable friend who is malicious and jealous
Pony: Small but timely assistance from unexpected person
Porcupine: A delicate embarrassment in public places
Porpoise: An evasive but bitter enemy tries to harm
Rabbit (black): Inconsistency in everything
Rabbit (running): Disappointment in many areas of life
Rabbit (white): Pure friendship will help under stress
Ram: An obstacle to overcome by hard work
Ram (butted by): A loss of respect or position
Rat: A greedy or sly foe interrupts happiness
Rat (swarm): Serious attack by bold enemies over lover
Rhinoceros: Very good business conditions
Rhinoceros (sickly): Most unfavorable for lovers or newlyweds

Seal: A true and lovely friend comes to assist
Sheep (dead): Sorrow over friends or business associates
Sheep (good condition): Much comfort in every way to come
Sheep (lean and dirty): Poverty which can be overcome by work
Sheep (shearing): Success after much difficulty
Sheep (shorn): Losses and delays in affairs of the heart
Skunk: A very sensitive friend may become an enemy
Squirrel: Quarrels and opposition from unexpected places
Stag: A noble friend stands by to help
Stag (attacked by): Proud and honorable foe will cause trouble
Stallion: Great honor and advancement in business
Tiger: Bitter enemy of great influence creates anguish
Weasel: An unprincipled adviser, probably an attorney
Whale: Great danger to strike when not expected
Wolf: A cruel, crafty, and avaricious individual
Wolf (bitten by): Badly cheated by someone you love and respect
Wolf (killing): Overcoming schemes of a greedy person
Zebra: Mixture of good and bad fortune in near future
Zoo: Many tiresome matters and plenty of gossip

CHAPTER 5

Birds

All through the ages . . . people have regarded their dreams as sources of wisdom, guidance and insight.

Rollo May

Birds are usually a preferred symbol, especially in matters of love, passion, and domestic tranquility. However, when the birds appear sickly or weak, the dreamer should expect discontent, disillusionment, and frustration.

If birds are seen flying north and the sky is clear, success is predicted for all endeavors. If, instead, they fly south, depression or a dull, unexciting sense of boredom will envelop the dreamer. If the sky looks stormy when the birds fly over, the future is discouraging. If they happen to be feeding, expect some good things to take place. But should they be fighting, it represents unhappiness and disagreement between close friends. Mating birds always indicate marital bliss and luck in all love matters.

Killing any birds denoting something good signifies unexpected cruelty in the dreamer's life. However, if the birds being killed signify a bad omen in the first place, it is a sign of overcoming any problems the dreamer may be having with a rival. Catching a bird in a dream is a premonition of a wedding. But if a wild bird is caught and then confined in a cage, there will be little marital bliss.

Napoleon

The births of many notable warriors and conquerors were foretold in dreams experienced by their mothers. For example, just before Napoleon I was born, his mother dreamed that she gave birth to a soaring eagle. This was interpreted to mean her forthcoming child would become extremely famous and that he would hold a high position of leadership.

Singing birds portend much happiness. This is especially true when the dreamer clearly hears a lark. Birds heard chirping at night are dire warnings of sadness and problems to come. The exception to this rule is the nightingale, or the woodcock when singing in the moonlight. Passion and unsurpassed love are indicated.

Dead birds seen in a dream always signify disappointment and sadness in all areas of life, but especially in love affairs and marriage.

The surroundings here, as with all other dream symbols, play a very important part in interpretations. If birds are seen flying around on a sunny day, in a garden or perched on a shrub, contentment and joy can be expected. But, if seen flying around in a storm, in a barren tree or a lifeless field, there is much misfortune coming.

Aigrette: Vanity and stupidity will hurt you
Bird (catching one): Marriage in the near future
Bird (dead): Great sorrow in store
Bird (flying about): Happiness in everything
Brood: Simple pleasures satisfy needs
Black bird: Gossip and scandal will hurt feelings
Blue bird: Happiness from new friends and lovers
Buzzard: Revengeful and malicious enemies
Cage: Loss of freedom
Cage (empty): Loss of love
Canary: A loving and devoted friend will help
Chicken: Good news of profit is on the way
Cock: Beware of boasting to associates
Crow: Failure of expectations in all areas of life
Cuckoo: Inconsistency of a loved one will cause harm
Dove: Love and contentment in immediate future
Duck: Thrift and material gain
Duck (wild): Fortunate journeys will be taken
Eagle: Victory with honors and great social status
Eggs: Happiness and wealth forthcoming soon
Eggs (broken): Lawsuits and other trouble
Eggs (rotten): Disgrace and dishonor
Falcon: Victory over all rivals if careful

Feather (black): Sorrow around lover and friends
Feather (gray): Consolation from new friend
Feather (rose): Pure love in relationship
Feather (white): Pure happiness in marital life
Feather (yellow): Wealth to come soon
Goose: Wealth and good cheer for next year
Goose (cackling): Warning of enemies close at hand
Hawk: Avaricious enemy making a move
Hen: Profit and good news in immediate future
Jay: A greedy neighbor to steal expensive item
King bird: A protecting friend who loves you
Kingfisher: Unexpected good luck helps in a pinch
Kite: A bitter foe looking for revenge
Lark: Success if you can rise to it and hold it
Lovebirds: Happiness in marriage when cautious
Magpie: An amusing situation causes problems
Magpie (more than one): Serious evil influences
Mocking bird: Some musical entertainment lifts spirits
Nest (empty): Disappointment and heartache
Nest (filled): Much good luck
Nightingale: Glorious love and happiness in affairs and marriage
Ostrich: Misadventure through vanity and trouble through greed
Owl: Warning of trouble, beware of false friends
Peacock: Conquest in love. Luck in marriage
Pelican: A mixture of good and bad news
Pheasant: Unusual good luck. Expect breaks
Pigeon: Reconciliation with long-absent friend
Quail: Contentment in home life and love matters
Quill: *See* Feather
Raven: Misfortune and possible theft, other troubles
Sparrow: Loving but quarrelsome friends, heartache
Stork: News of a birth, general bliss
Stork (two together): A marriage, possible marvelous affair
Swallow: News from the absent, long-lost friend returns
Swan (black): Something unexpected to happen

Swan (white): Wealth and honors bestowed shortly
Turkey: Abundance and good cheer, plenty of friends
Vulture: An intriguing enemy will move in and cause distress
Wings: *See* Feather
Wren: A faithful mate and devoted mother, good marriage

CHAPTER 6

Precious Stones and Jewelry

One of the most adventurous things left us is to go to bed. For no one can lay a hand on our dreams.

E. V. Lucas

Any rare, valuable, or beautiful piece of jewelry, or a precious stone, is to be taken as a sign of great favor. The dreamer is warned to be careful if the item happens to be cracked, broken, or disfigured in any manner. In this condition it denotes a loss of friendship, broken love affair, or a divided marriage. However, if the stone or jewelry can be repaired, there is a good chance for lovers to make amends.

If the jewelry or stone is seen to be blemished or even badly tarnished, but it can be repaired or cleaned, carelessness has caused the problems. This may readily be reversed through more thoughtfulness.

An imperfection in any stone or piece of jewelry indicates unhappiness, disgust, and fraud. Any stone attached to a setting which must be pinned on the clothing presages sadness and discontent. If the point is bent, then this state of affairs will not be long-lasting.

An interesting example of a dream involving a precious stone is that of the Missouri farmer who lived outside of St. Louis. One night, while fast asleep, a young girl appeared in his dream and took his hand in hers. She quietly led him to an old wooden fence and pointed to a huge ruby laying on the ground in front of one of the posts. She then whispered in his ear: "Come here tomorrow and look for a beautiful reddish stone. Pick it up carefully and set it aside." The girl suddenly disappeared.

The farmer, upon arising in the morning, went out in his pasture to search for the stone seen in his dream. He spotted a large rock with a red hue. Upon rolling the stone away from the area, he found a small metal box underneath in a hole. The box turned out to be filled with old gold coins—a gift from the girl in his dream.

Agate: Long and healthy life
Beads (counting): Contentment and fun-filled future
Beads (scattering): Trouble and vexation to be expected
Beads (sharp edges): Unpleasant associates cause trouble
Beads (smooth and round): Happy friendships and social activities
Beads (stringing): Gain in some pleasant way, happy times
Bloodstone: Courage always brings success in everything
Bracelet: Completion of love conquest
Bracelet (wearing): A happy union, good marriage or affair
Brooch: A pleasant affair in the near future
Brooch (a gift): Something sad to happen
Brooch (mourning): Tears over great losses or death
Cameo: A beautiful love affair, meeting a new lover
Carnelian: Protection from worry and bad influences
Chain: Links of close friendship more solidified
Chain (broken): Loss of friend or some close relative
Charm: Unusual good luck if cautious
Chrysolite: Preservation from effects of sensuality
Combs: Attention and admiration of friends and associates
Combs (of tortoiseshell): Expect envious friends
Coral: Protection from illness or harm, bad influences
Crown: *see* Chapter 18
Diadem: Great honors, possibly overwhelming
Diamond: Wealth and happiness throughout life
Diamond (from a lover): A wealthy marriage or profitable affair
Diamond (lose): Disaster coming

Earrings: Good news shared by a friend
Earrings (broken): Gossip and malicious friends
Earrings (black): News of a death in the family
Emblems (of a secret order): Honor and protection in everything
Emerald: Wealth, health, and a long trip
Emerald (with a pin attachment): Envy and jealousy for lovers
Fob (with initial): New friend to offer aid
Fob (worn by a woman): A new lover immediately
Gems: *See* individual stones, otherwise it is a sign of wealth
Girdle (if ornamental): Social pleasures forthcoming
Girdle (if useful): Warm, consoling love and new endeavors
Gold: *See* Chapter 21
Jade: Great good luck and protection from evil deeds of others
Jasper: Protection from evil influences. Success in business
Lapis Lazuli: Truth protects against evil designs of enemies
Locket: Someone who never forgets you. A lover who cares
Locket (antique): An inheritance is overdue
Lorgnette: Friendly advice of great value
Necklace: Happy love and marriage unless the stones are unfavorable symbols
Necklace (broken): Unhappiness and separation in love or marriage
Onyx: Protection from all bad influences
Onyx (black): Loss of a loved one
Opal: Hope in spite of changing fortune, expect good things
Pearl: Good fortune in love and social activities
Pearl (breaking string): Unhappiness, especially in sexual things
Pearl (from a lover): Happy marriage and good lovers
Pearl (losing): Loss of lover or death of marriage partner
Pin (blunt point): Trouble through lack of money
Pin (hat): Protection from unpleasant associates
Pin (scarf): Danger in all social activities
Ring: Happy love affairs with many partners
Ring (broken): Broken engagement or marriage split
Ring (wedding): Impending marriage
Ruby: Wealth and love successes
Sapphire: Peace and wisdom in all things, great bliss

Sleeve links: Happy union in love or marriage, new lovers
Sleeve links (broken): Trouble in business matters
Sleeve links (gift): Happy love affair or marriage
Sleeve links (lost): Loss of a lover or a mate
Studs (bright): Domestic comfort and happiness
Studs (broken): Much annoyance
Studs (lost): Much trouble brewing
Studs (tarnished): Unhappiness and discomfort can't be avoided
Topaz: Faithful and staunch friends will support
Topaz (lost): Envy makes trouble for lovers and friends
Turquoise: Sincere friends and success with lovers

CHAPTER 7

Flowers, Vegetables, Herbs, and Grains

> **I am interested in the effect dreams may have upon our lives. . . . I would like to know how my dreaming shapes (if it does) my life.**
>
> ***Jessamyn West***

Flowers always presage devoted love, sincere affection, continuous bliss, and free-flowing passions in all personal relationships. Blooming, fragrant, and lovely, they denote everything good. When wilted in a pot or on the stem, they portend passion and sexual experiences soon to be forgotten. Gathering flowers in a dream means success in finding a lover and much joy while together. Seeing a couple of flowers amid the weeds denotes but very little sensual pleasure although the individual exerts much effort in this direction. Dried rose petals or other dried flowers always presage fond memories of past lovers and former sensual experiences.

Fresh, crisp vegetables always denote good health. Enjoyment of simple, everyday things is also evidenced. If the vegetables are wilted, there will be many problems caused through thoughtlessness and oversight. If bruised or rotting, even more problems are foretold—these because of ignorance and procrastination. Gathering vegetables in a dream denotes the saving of money and abundant material things. Placing fresh vegetables in a basket, bag, or box presages a speedy marriage for singles. It also foretells of domestic tranquillity for married couples.

Dreams of herbs portend continuing excellent health for well people. Those who are sick will quickly recover. Relief will come to those in pain, or those who suffer mental anguish. If the herbs are wilted, they portend sadness and distress through neglect of the dreamer's health. Dreaming of dried herbs indicates that the individual has provided well for the future.

Grains always presage abundance of material goods and great success in all areas of life. If ears of corn are very full and appear rich, then things in life will be bountiful. Ears of corn appearing haggard denote poverty or at least great need because of laziness and inaction. Entire fields of healthy grain in a dream express huge monetary gains, and enduring peace of mind.

Gardens with healthy, green-looking plants represent great opportunity for love, happiness, and material gain. If the plants are seen to be mature, a rosy and solid future are predicted. Newly budding garden plants portend a happy, well-matched marriage for lovers. If the plants are leafless, or sickly, there will be very little love and lack of mental peace for the time being.

"The conception of the dream that was held in prehistoric ages by primitive peoples," declares Sigmund Freud, "and the influence it may have exerted on the formation of their conception of the universe, and of the soul, is a theme of such great interest that it is only with great reluctance that I refrain from dealing with it . . ."

Anise: All sorrow and pain to be released
Arbutus: A very sweet lover who is shy
Artichoke: Something embarrassing is soon to happen
Aster (purple): An elderly, wealthy friend will assist
Aster (white): True love will envelop the dreamer
Azalea: Happiness and success will long endure
Balm of Gilead: Both the body and the mind will heal
Barley: Good health with many comforts to come
Basil: Hurt feelings to be healed by the truth
Beans: Family quarrels cause much friction

Beets: No need to fret. All worries to disappear
Bluebell: Shy but devoted friends abound to assist
Bouquet: An offering of love from someone least expected
Buckwheat: Unexpected wealth from new source
Buttercup: Riches and much joy in life
Cabbage: A long and happy life with a good mate
Camellia: Intense love and devotion
Caraway: An amusing problem to overcome
Carnation: A true and very clever friend will help
Catnip: A true and very independent friend fails in time of need
Celery: Prosperity and honors for friends and lovers
Celery (decayed): Illness in the family can be expected
Chrysanthemum (colored): Deep love and much wealth
Chrysanthemum (white): Spiritual growth forthcoming
Clover: Success through ingenuity and hard work
Columbine: Determination brings success to those who try
Coriander: A delightful romance is a surprise
Corn: Increase in fortune or family, good news received
Cornflower: Quiet but devoted friends in abundance
Cotton: Great changes for the better
Cucumber: Recovery for the sick. Glad tidings
Daffodil: Happiness through faithfulness in marriage
Dahlia: Great good fortune from new friends
Daisy: Health and innocent gaiety promised
Daisy (out of season): Disappointment and sadness
Endive: Good results through wise economy
Fennel: A humble but devoted friend to offer aid
Fern: Consolation when in trouble
Forget-me-not: Meeting of old friends or lovers
Garlic: Important secrets disclosed when most needed
Geranium: A happy love affair is coming, possible marriage
Goldenrod: Pride and wealth for honest associates
Goldenrod (stunted): Care only for wealth
Grass (frozen or dried): Loneliness or distress foretold
Grass (green and luxuriant): A happy, full life
Hay: Influential friends assist in success, meet new lovers
Hemp: Success in everything to be expected
Hollyhock: Ambition wins the day, gain of cash

Honeysuckle: Sweet and ardent love from surprise source
Iris: A very desirable love affair will influence life
Jessamine: Joy, but not lasting and early marriage for lovers
Lavender: Consolation of sweet memories and fond dreams
Lentils: Disagreeable conditions to overcome, success rules
Lettuce: Health and many good things, financial gain
Lilac: Happiness in love and life, small irritations
Lilies: Purification through sorrow, heartbreak
Lilies (out of season): Disappointment, broken limb
Lilies (withered): Discontentment, displeasure with friends
Lilies (with rich foliage): Early marriage, new problems
Marigolds: Jealousy or envy of wealth, ambition will harm
Marjoram: An embarrassing incident, private meetings
Melon: Health and recovery of the sick, new endeavors
Mints: Spicy adventures, sensuality problems
Moss: Lack of independence causes a delay in progress
Mushrooms: Unhealthy desires cause sadness and problems
Mustard: Success and wealth foreseen
Myrtle: Declaration or acceptance of love by new conquest
Narcissus: Vanity causes much sorrow. Beware of new enemy
Nettles: Lack of many material things
Oats: A variety of good things, positive news
Onion: An unpleasant truth revealed, be careful
Pansy: Contentment in love, much bliss
Parsley: Hard-earned successes, new tasks
Parsnips: Favorable for all affairs except love and marriage
Peas: Very good fortune, financial gain expected
Pennyroyal: Virtue rewarded when least expected, new lover
Peony: Wealth and enjoyment soon to come
Peppers: Steadfastly claim your rights of monetary nature
Poppies: Idle talk and gossip will cause harm
Pot herbs: Disclosure of family secrets, great embarrassment
Primrose: Inconsistency, rely on no one
Primrose (yellow): Jealousy will cause problems
Pumpkin: Abundance and good cheer follow good deed
Radish: A secret unexpectedly revealed by close friend
Rhubarb: Health and happy reconciliation for friends
Rice: Abundance in all things necessary for happy life

Rose (bud): A new friend or lover to enter life
Rose (gathering): An opportunity for marriage, be careful
Rose (moss): Tender but shy affection, enjoyment of everything
Rose (petals falling): Hopes departing, try a new area
Rose (pink): Happy love and blissful relationships
Rose (red): Ardent love to overwhelm you
Rose (spotted or mildewed): An unfortunate love affair
Rose (white): Constant and true love
Rose (withered or dead): Departure of loved one, bad news
Rose (yellow): jealous lover
Rosebush (with blossoms): Unlimited joy
Rosebush (with buds): Happiness which will increase
Rosebush (withered): Loss of a loved one, sadness to come
Rosemary: Happiness in remembrance, new endeavor will succeed
Rue: Danger from false pride and unchecked lust
Saffron: Danger near at hand, be careful with new friends
Saffron (wilted or withered): Danger will be overcome
Sage: Gain in esteem of friends, prestige on job
Seeds: You will reap what you sow—Beware! Danger lurking
Snowball: Happiness and bliss in love, expect good things
Sorrel: Quarrels and contention among friends
Spinach: Health gained with a little effort
Squash: Gain in wealth and health, many other lucky things
Straw: Approaching poverty can be avoided with care
Summer savory: A wise and happy life with a good partner
Sunflower: Glowing happiness and ardent love comes soon
Sweet peas: Tender love and gaiety to be experienced
Thistle: Difficulties overcome by firmness and help of others
Thorns: Opposition from enemies to be expected
Thyme: Energy brings eventual success
Tomatoes: Enjoyment and entertainment from surprising places
Tuberose: Depression and loneliness may overwhelm you
Tulips: Happiness in love for all if discreet and honest
Turnips: Prospects will improve in every way, much luck
Turnips (wilted): Cure for the very ill
Vines: *See* Chapter 3
Water lily: Out of deep sorrow some happiness will arise

CHAPTER 8

Insects, Fish, and Reptiles

And it was so, when Gideon heard the telling of the dream, and the interpretation thereof, that he worshipped and returned into the host of Israel. . . .

Judges, 7:15

Insects seen in a dream are seldom good omens. They denote minor problems and irritants. There are some exceptions to this rule: the ant, bee, cricket. Lice and other vermin usually denote a gain of cash, but sometimes they are a warning of impending sickness.

Reptiles are unlucky omens to see in dreams. They normally warn of animosity from friends, deceit in the dreamer's daily life, and of selfish enemies surrounding the dreamer.

Shellfish (crabs, lobster, and so forth) are not signs of good fortune. Most other kinds of fish are portents of luck and better times. Fish being caught in a dream denote many good things to come through the efforts of the dreamer. Dead fish indicate nothing more or less than severe disillusionment and lots of disappointment in love and in business matters.

"Like some letters in a cipher," reports J. Sully, "the dream inscription when scrutinized closely loses its first look of balderdash and takes on the aspect of a serious, intelligible message. Or, to vary the figure slightly, we may say that, like some palimpsest the dream discloses beneath its worthless surface—character traces of an old and precious communication."

Alligator: A malicious enemy and false friends
Ant: Hard work will bring grand achievements
Bed bugs: Illness and sadness to enter life
Bedbugs (failure to kill): Danger from enemies and others
Bee: Profit and increase of everything
Bee (killing): Great losses and possible ruin resulting from enemy
Bee (swarms): Great wealth for sincere acts
Beetle: Miseries and disagreeable conditions
Boa constrictor: Great danger from a powerful individual
Bugs: Meddlesome friends who are harmless
Butterfly: Fleeting pleasures of a sensual nature
Butterfly (catching): Happiness destroyed by unfaithful lover
Butterfly (chasing): A foolish fancy for someone in family
Caterpillar: Slander because of envy to engulf dreamer
Clams: Sorrow through dumb lack of compassion
Crabs: Affairs will go against your desires
Crawfish: Little gain for efforts in life and love
Cricket: Contentment amid happy surroundings assured
Crocodile: A false friend or hateful relative
Earthworms: Secret adversaries seek your ruination and demise
Eel: Danger from irresponsible friends and dangerous foes
Fish (empty net): Loss of fortune
Fish (full net): Increase of fortune
Fish (hooks): Deception and entanglements are forthcoming

Flea: Irritations caused by ill-will of friend or relative
Flea (dead): Inconsistency for those in love
Fly: Exasperation caused by ridiculous activities
Fly (horse): Persecution from a close friend
Frog: Beware of flattery given falsely
Goldfish: Luxury and pleasure are in store
Grasshopper: Losses and much disappointment for lovers
Herring: Increase in family or stock, expect good things
Leeches: Avaricious associates or relatives, new enemies
Lice: Plenty of money but much annoyance
Lizard: A warning of the advance of a secret enemy
Lobster: A silly and temperamental love affair
Locust: Greedy relatives and associates will hurt you
Mackerel: Friendly assistance toward success is destined
Moth (indoor): Losses through employees or close friends
Moth (outdoor): Dangerous flirtations to cause problems
Mosquito: Malicious and meddlesome friends
Mullet: Serious illness of a close friend or relative
Mussels: Contentment with very little. Expect a surprise
Oysters: Feasting and plenty soon to arrive
Salamander: A bitter enemy of some influence and much power
Salmon: Good luck and pleasant surroundings at home
Sardines: Unpleasant domestic affairs, bad investments
Scorpion: Attempts to take advantage of good nature
Serpent: Dangerous deception by supposed friend
Shark: A dangerous enemy who may be ferocious
Shrimp: Grief over actions of a lover and a friend
Silkworm: A charitable friend with powerful connections
Snail: An honorable position over many others
Snake: *See* Serpent
Spider: Conquest of all difficulties through work
Tadpole: A doubtful affair and bad business deal
Tapeworm: Very favorable for increased wealth and bliss
Tarantula: A bitter enemy to strike
Tarantula (killing): Success after much struggling
Toad: Something unpleasant will turn out for the good
Tortoise: A secret enemy to make himself known

Turtle: Improvement slow but certain
Vermin: Enough of everything but bad health
Wasp: Insolence from someone respected
Whale: Great danger from unexpected source
Worms: Secret enemies in your midst, possible illness

CHAPTER 9

People

And what else is one to believe, if not what dreams tell one. . . .

Eugene Ionesco

A crowd of happy people, or a group of fun-loving friends is always a positive sign. This indicates cooperation in business matters, a big gain in social stature, and abundance of pleasures in life. Children seen happily playing in a dream or teenagers dancing at a party signifies bliss and total peace of mind just around the corner. Dreaming of a riot or any other noisy situation, denotes involvement in political events and erratic finances. If the people seen in a riot are sickly looking, expect much distress, sickness, and other depressing things.

Drusus was given command of the Roman army during the

Drusus

Augustus

German war, and was left a free hand by Emperor Augustus. The night prior to his crossing the Elbe, he went to sleep and had an unusual dream. A lovely woman appeared before him and spoke in a low, sensuous voice: "Whither goest thou so fast, oh, Drusus? Art thou never tired of conquest? Know, then, that thy days are at an end."

Drusus was disturbed by the words heard in his dream and pondered the problem the next morning. He decided to order a general retreat, even though he had been successful in his past battle exploits. Drusus gave the order, his armies were overrun, and he perished immediately thereafter on the banks of the bloody Rhine.

"No one ever dreams nonsense! A dream which one remembers so distinctly that one can relate it afterwards, and which," declares Lynkus, "therefore, is no dream of delirium, *always* has a meaning; why, it cannot be otherwise."

Working people busily engaged in some enterprise predict successful achievement in everything attempted. When these same people are seen as lazy or lethargic, or if simply dissatisfied, then expect financial problems.

Ministers or priests signify unsurpassed lust and ambition. Dishonor and unhappiness are in store for the dreamer. Any dream of people attending church presages problems in the social arena. The dreamer's conduct must be guarded.

Unapproving brothers or sisters appearing in a dream signify arguments and hostility. Scolding mothers and fathers appearing in a dream denote dissension and stress. Other chiding relatives denote impending trouble. Stepbrothers or stepsisters seen in a dream are indicative of a problem with an inheritance, and arguments over personal possessions.

Dreaming of deceased relatives is covered under Dead People, Chapter 19.

If a dream portends a good omen, yet there is something uncomfortable felt, deceit is forthcoming. When the deceased present an unfavorable omen, yet the dreamer feels good, it signifies that good will result from any misfortune encountered. This can be verified only by considering all the other things seen in the dream. When everything in the dream appears to be good, but the dreamer senses anxiety, disappointment should be expected.

Acrobat: Exciting adventures lie ahead in life
Actor: Improvement in general health
Actress: Improvement in wealth and fortune
Adventurer: Beware of all easy money schemes
Artist: Deception in love affairs and other areas of life
Assassin: Expect to be spared new and unpleasant things
Baby (carriage): Pleasant surprises are in store
Baby (clean and happy): Faithful and affectionate friends
Baby (crying or sickly): Abundant temporary stress
Baby (holding): No pressure to conform by your lover
Baby (nursing): Look for deceit to some degree
Baby (rocking): Embarrassment over something
Bachelor: Beware of intrigues with the opposite sex
Barber: Loss of health in a short time
Beggar: Family losses or other troubles
Burglar: Conquest over all foes
Burglar (if one): Reverses in business and love
Butcher: Great trouble and danger coming
Captain: Ambition gratified through a stranger
Carpenter: Progress in all affairs
Cavalry: On the road to accomplishment and success
Chambermaid: Valuable time wasted with gossip
Child (happy): Much contentment and pleasure
Child (playing with): Much success in everything
Child (unhappy or crying): Many vexations
Clairvoyant: Unpleasant things will hinder success
Clergyman: *See* Minister
Clerk: Small returns but a pleasant occupation
Clown: Bitter disappointment, especially in love matters
Cobbler: A possible failure avoided by a wise decision
Convict: Disaster and terrible news
Crew: Expected trip will be prevented
Criminal: Unscrupulous friends or relatives to take advantage
Dentist: Associates lack honor and sincerity
Detective: A warning to be cautious

Doctor (as friend): Improvement in all ways
Doctor (professionally): Dissension and sickness
Driver: Opportunity is all around the dreamer
Druggist: Doubtful fun and pleasure
Dwarf: An attack by a petty foe
Enemy: Serious cause for mistrust
Engineer: Happy meeting as a result of a long trip
Executioner: Business failure
Family: Illness or distress will soon appear if any member is seen this way in a dream
Fisherman: Prosperity can be expected quite soon
Fortune-teller: Worry with no real cause
Friends: Expect a letter with good tidings
Guardian: Friends will show much kindness and understanding
Gypsy: Deception in love and other affairs
Harlot: Actions will end in a major scandal
Housekeeper: Domestic comforts and happiness
Hunchback: An unlucky omen unless dreamer touches hump
Husband: Quarrels followed by making up and having fun
Husband (dead): Disappointment and much deception
Husband (loved by a single girl): Lack of love and attention
Husband (loving another's): Unhappy marriage and no fidelity
Husband (loving another woman): Infidelity soon to show itself
Imbecile: Humiliation in private. Lacking of funds
Invalid: Disagreeable situations and people
Janitor: Many petty annoyances
Jester: Opportunity lost through pursuit of pleasure
Jockey: Rash speculation brings great losses
Judge: The law will decide all disputes
King: *See* Royalty
Knife grinder: Malicious interference breeds problems
Lawyer: Misunderstandings will be adjusted quickly
Leper: Sorrow caused by scandalous behavior
Lodger: Opposite sex will cause usual problems
Lover (angry): Unhappiness in wedded state
Lover (happy): Ardent love affairs
Lover (indifferent): Loss of feeling for lover

Man (healthy): Bliss and untold good things to happen
Man (many together): Something important is going to take place
Man (old): Lack of luck and little persistence
Man (unhealthy): Disgrace and dishonor, bad luck
Man (wounded): Reputation lost for good
Mason: hard work but little success
Midwife: Delightful news of some kind
Miller: Present conditions to improve
Miner: No success in spite of forceful efforts
Minister: Disagreeable experiences, a bad omen all around
Miser: An unexpected gift or inheritance
Missionary: Dissension and irritations
Model: Worries and intrigues, a poor sign for lovers
Monk: A false friend will be seen through
Monk (with a hood): Reconciliation with loved ones
Musician: Contentment and much pleasure
Neighbor: Dangerous gossip should be avoided
Nobility: *See* Royalty
Notary: Lawsuits and general dissatisfaction
Nun: An untrustworthy woman friend, separation for lovers
Nun (to become one): Unhappiness is in store
Nurse: Much illness caused through carelessness
Occultist: Accept blame for lack of responsibility
Officer (army): No advancement and little success
Officer (navy): Unsuccessful endeavors, unfortunate trip
Officer (police): Caution required in all activities
Orator: Beware of saying too much
Orphan: Estrangement from relatives and friends
Page: Business partner to quit, mate may leave
Pallbearer: Much sorrowful news, a bad omen always
Passenger (arriving): An improvement in luck, financial gain
Passenger (leaving): Money disappointments
Pawnbroker: Little success for hard work
Physician: *See* Doctor
Pirate: A very fortunate omen, much adventure
Pope: A warning to be more careful and considerate
Porter: Assistance of someone unexpectedly

Postman: News from a friend far away
Preacher: *See* Minister
Priest: A need for a change of outlook, unfavorable for those who happen to be sick or prisoners
Printer: Idleness breeds poverty, be careful
Prostitute: Censure for ill-advised actions
Quaker: Faithful lover and fine friends, possible success
Queen: *See* Royalty
Reaper (busy): Prosperity comes soon, expect everything
Reaper (idle): Dull times in love and business
Regiment: Quarrels with all, little mental peace
Reporter: Scandalous secrets revealed by a friend
Rival: Misfortune in love, a change of luck for the worst
Robber: Danger of love and business losses
Rogue: Indiscretion will cause problems with boss
Royalty: A sign of ambition and forcefulness
Royalty (censured by): Conduct causes great disgrace
Royalty (receiving favors from): Many honors, success
Sailor: News from distant lands
Scholar: Deceit in an apparently good idea
Schoolteacher: Professional success
Sculptor: Distinction but little money
Seamstress: Disappointment regarding a trip or visit
Sentry: Protection from all danger or an enemy
Servant: Annoyance from petty gossip
Servant (to be one): Lack of any self-respect
Shepherd: Success will require much prudence
Sheriff: Business matters require precautions
Sheriff (to be one): Unfavorable for going into business
Socialist: Affairs neglected by an abundance of talk
Soldiers: Depression and problem situations unavoidable
Spy: Suspicious activities on part of a friend
Stenographer (firing one): Many unexpected fights
Stenographer (hiring): Expanding business matters
Stranger: Unexpected assistance from a stranger
Sweetheart: Happiness in love, problems with associates
Tailor: Quarrels and contention over money
Tramp: Dangerous companions and idleness

Traveler: Meeting many old friends, good times ahead
Waiter: Some very pleasant news and entertainment
Washerwoman: Dissipation and irritations
Watchman: Security lacking, be on guard
Widow, widower: Much intrigue, trust no one
Wife (angry): Jangled nerves and a multitude of bad things
Wife (happy): Success in all undertakings
Wife (weeping): Great distress and sadness to come
Woman (beautiful): Happiness in love life
Woman (many): A social affair, much gossip
Woman (old): Many unreasonable demands
Woman (ugly): Too much nagging

CHAPTER 10

Clothing

Do ye know the terror of him who falleth asleep?—to the very toes he is terrified, because the ground giveth way under him, and the dream beginneth.
Friedrich Nietzsche

The general condition (new, used, clean, dirty, torn, and so forth) of clothing worn in a dream helps in the overall interpretation. Also important is the sensation the dreamer feels when touching or seeing clothing. New clothing which brings much pleasure is a sign of happiness and monetary gain. Filthy or soiled clothing signifies humiliation, disgrace, and some degree of infamy. When clothes are torn, attacks on the dreamer's character and reputation are to take place. Clothing that is too heavy denotes that the dreamer spends too much time on outward appearances. Not enough thought is given to emotional development. When the clothing is seen as clean but well-worn or threadbare, a shortage of money is presaged. Bad judgment is seen to be the major cause of the problem.

Uncomfortable hats or scarves, or ill-fitting head attire presage that the dreamer is ill at ease because of temporary present conditions or circumstances. All unhappiness will soon be eliminated. When a hat or head covering is too tight, obstacles to success stand in the way. A hat overly large portends a great need for more forethought when ready to take action. Haste must be delayed in order to take better advantage of new opportunities.

When a piece of clothing is seen as a favorable omen, but uncomfortable to wear, expect to be deceived by a friend or business associate. Where an unfavorable omen-bearing piece of clothing makes the dreamer feel good, lying and misleading advice will be freely given. A piece of clothing bearing an unlucky connotation, and feeling uncomfortable to the dreamer, denotes problems and discontent. Exceptions to this rule would be clothing easily taken off: aprons, hats, gloves, and so forth. These items reveal that the dreamer can easily overcome obstacles. Wearing too few clothes, or being naked in a dream presages humiliation for the dreamer.

"As regards the dream," offers philosopher Edward von Hartmann, "with it all the troubles of waking life pass over into the sleeping state; all save the one thing which may in some degree reconcile the cultured person with life—scientific and artistic enjoyment."

Apron: Ups and downs of fortune to be quite regular
Baby clothing: Good news and a surprise forthcoming
Belt (cloth): A stranger to soon come into your life
Belt (frayed): New friends to be mistrusted
Belt (leather): Financial gain through friends
Blouse (clean): Happiness in everything

Blouse (dainty): Joyous meetings with others
Blouse (silk): Riches and new social status
Blouse (soiled): Disgraceful gossip and lies abound
Blouse (torn): A number of illicit love affairs
Blouse (trying on): A great rivalry for the one loved
Boots (army): Travels throughout the world
Boots (loose): Problems while traveling
Boots (rubber): Little success in life, expect discomforts
Boots (too tight): Be on guard against fraud
Bridal costume (happy in): A large inheritance coming
Bridal costume (soiled): Great unhappiness in marriage, hatred
Bridal costume (unhappy in): Disappointment in some expected pleasure, it will cause great sorrow
Buttons: Good cheer and domestic comforts, friend will aid
Buttons (missing): Something embarrassing will happen
Cap: Some event of no great importance will surprise you
Chemise: Disagreeable gossip will excite the mind
Collar: Honor and distinction, unfavorable for women
Corset: Perplexities and opposition, faithless friend
Dress (evening): Many exciting love affairs
Dress (house): Domestic happiness and contentment
Dress (street): Business experience, also trouble brewing
Dress (night): Slight illness, stalwart friends
Dressing (with ease): Social progress, content with self
Dressing (with difficulty): Envy interferes with success
Feathers: *See* Chapter 5
Furs (rich and glossy): Luxury will come to you
Furs (worn or soiled): Ungratified ambition, serious quirks
Gaiters: Amusements and rivalries, opposite sex will harm
Garters: Proposal of marriage for lovers, disgraceful affairs for married couples
Girdle (new): Honors and love, great luck in everything
Girdle (old): Hard work and troubles, luck will change
Gloves: A new friend of great influence
Gloves (losing): Loss of good friends, desertion by a loved one
Gown: *See* Dress
Handbag (handsome and full): Abundance of everything
Handbag (worn or empty): Extravagance will ruin chances

Handkerchief: A flirtation which leads to an affair
Handkerchief (losing): Loss of a lover, a possible accident
Handkerchief (torn): Broken engagement, bad investment
Handkerchief (waving): Behavior causes censure, serious mistakes
Hat (loose-fitting): Rivalry in social activities and love
Hat (too tight): Loss of love and prestige to a rival
Hat (trying on): Expect to meet new rival
Hood: Deception practiced by wearer, be on guard
Mantilla: Deception and intrigues, danger to the dreamer
Mourning: Bad luck and much unhappiness, a sign of very serious misunderstandings for lovers
Muff: A spicy life with plenty of everything
Overalls: Deception by person trusted with secrets
Overcoat (new): Success in everything
Overcoat (old): Difficulties caused by jealous mate
Parasol: Flirtation which causes grief
Parasol (walking under): An engagement, hopeful thoughts
Petticoat: An embarrassing situation, angry opposition
Ribbons: Social prestige, competition for lovers
Ribbons (wearing many): Frivolity causes sorrow for many
Sash: Flirtations cause problems—beware
Shawl: Attention from the opposite sex
Shirt (clean): Happiness may be expected, profit in business
Shirt (dirty): Illness coming
Shirt (losing): Disgrace through personal acts
Shirt (removing): False hopes with no results
Shoes: A journey very soon, may win a free trip
Shoes (losing): Distress over great losses
Shoes (new): Honor and much profit
Shoes (newly shined): Improvement in everything
Shoes (old): Actions bring much dishonor
Slippers (man's): Comfort and self-satisfaction
Slippers (woman's): Social pleasures to come soon
Socks: Contentment and all the comforts
Socks (with holes): Domestic unhappiness, bad luck generally
Stockings: A radical change in fortune
Tassels: Much success socially

Tassels (falling off): Unpleasant meeting with a friend
Trousers: Temptation to take advantage of opposite sex
Trousers (torn): Danger to reputation, be careful in crowds
Uniform (army): Honors and respect
Uniform (navy): Heroic deeds
Veil (black): Death or separation, unavoidable trouble
Veil (gray): Much misery in store
Veil (white): Offer of marriage, a questionable mate

CHAPTER 11

The Body

Some people do not sleep at all and constantly follow their problem while awake, others sleep but busy themselves with their plans in their dreams.

Alfred Adler

Healthy parts of the body seen in a dream are always a sign of happiness. Beautiful body parts are omens of great pleasure and satisfaction. There is only one exception: if the body part itself denotes a bad sign, the dreamer is going to face great temptation.

Ugly body parts, or an ugly face simply denotes bad luck and much sadness. Huge breasts seen on a woman, when they appear to be out of proportion to the rest of her body, suggest a gain of prestige and power. Well-developed muscles seen on a man or a woman in the nude also suggest more prestige and influence. Muscles on a person fully dressed denote the gain of social status and a possible inheritance. Areas of the body looking pleasantly plump, and somewhat sensuous, foretell of sensual pleasures in the near future.

Any part of the body that aches or feels painful presages illness. If any area is seen as infected or swollen, it is a warning of impending illness or a disease which can be avoided by taking proper precautions. This excludes the head. Aches or pains around the head are an omen of nervous breakdowns or impending mental or emotional problems.

Physical deformities seen in a dream warn of mental weakness and anguish over everything in life. The dreamer needs to be around cheerful and loving friends. If a physical or mental disability is seen in a dream, it denotes severe obstacles are in the way of eventual success.

Maldonat was a Jesuit who compiled a religious commentary on Matthew, Mark, Luke, and John. This man had an identical dream for four consecutive nights. An old-timer appeared and exhorted Maldonat to finish his work promptly. The old man assured him that he would complete the commentary, but that he would not live for long afterwards.

Each time the apparition made itself known in the dream, it would pick up a stick, dip it in a vat of blood, and proceed to make a "x" on Maldonat's stomach. Upon awakening, the Jesuit experienced severe pains. Jesuit Maldonat finished his writing task, and soon thereafter, died of terrible stomach cramps.

Abdomen: Many good opportunities to increase wealth
Abdomen (shrunken): Persecution by a number of false friends
Amputation (if ill): Relief from all agonies
Amputation (if well): Affliction of some sort to strike
Ankle (bony): Lover to cause minor problems
Ankle (bruised): Heartbreak around the corner
Ankle (inflamed): Problems to soon overcome dreamer
Ankle (smooth): Everything blissful and full of gain
Arms (beautiful): All love matters end well
Arms (clean): Happiness envelops the entire being
Arms (dirty): Much misery to overcome, and some troubles
Arms (hairy): Loads of endurance and strength
Arms (injured): Sadness which may be long-lasting
Back: Much misfortune and hard work in store
Back (bowed): Too much unwanted responsibility

Back (hunched): Spitefulness and maliciousness
Beard: Marriage for a single person, total control of financial affairs for married person, fortune will be especially good to a man
Beard (luxuriant): Most undertakings will be successful
Beard (shaving): Watch for grave misfortune
Beauty: Much affection and marvelous good fortune
Bitten (by animal): Enemy can be expected to attack
Bitten (by insect): Beware of dangerous gossip
Bitten (by person): An enemy seeking revenge
Bitten (by snake): A phony friend will harm you
Bladder (blown up): Do not build on false hopes
Blood: Caution required in all future dealings
Bones: Losses and great failure in something important
Brain: Worry will be the cause of problems
Breast (discolored): Sterility in either sex
Breast (full): Little illness and much happiness
Breast (hairy): Strength for men, lack of strength for women
Breast (shrunken): Health and love will be lost
Breast (wounded): Reputation to be ruined
Breath (sweet): Bliss and much affection
Breath (uneven): An exciting event
Breath (unpleasant): Sadness and possible sickness
Complexion (clear): Contentment and peace of mind
Complexion (freckled): Irritations will cause problems
Complexion (pimpled): Plenty of cash but many problems
Corpse: Grief and a death of someone dear
Corpse (many): A battle or fight with others
Cut: Expect friend or lover to be treacherous
Ears: Surprise information to soon arrive
Ears (extra): Problems created by nasty words
Ears (unable to hear): Refusal of friend's advice
Ears (waxy): Expect to succeed in all things
Ears (wounded): A secret will be told
Eyes (blind): Expect infidelity and some illness
Eyes (cross-eyed): Bad luck in almost everything
Eyes (one-eyed): To suffer astounding losses
Eyes (on guard): Protection from enemies

Eyes (single eye in space): Protection of all material goods
Eyes (squinting): Deception used against wishes
Eyebrows (luxuriant): Esteem of friends and associates
Eyebrows (sparse): Loss of reputation
Eyeglasses: Neighbor to be troublemaker
Eyeglasses (broken): Confusion to reign temporarily
Face (angry): Rage will bring on sickness
Face (haggard): Worry affects daily routine
Face (lovely): Happy, joyful, and full of affection
Face (pale): Neglect of health brings sickness
Face (sorrowful): A dire warning to change habits
Face (ugly): Actions ruled by bitterness
Fat: Prosperity and bliss to come
Feet (corns): Irritations and obstacles
Feet (dirty): Tribulations can be defeated
Feet (extra): An excellent omen for those who travel
Feet (shrunken): Changes for the worst
Feet (strong): Fun trips and successful ventures
Fingers: New lovers and gain of friends
Fingers (cut or injured): Loved ones will cause problems
Fingers (extra): A multitude of new acquaintances
Fingers (losing): Friends will desert you
Fingers (thumb very big): Much power and prestige
Fingers (withered): Sickness and loss of money
Fingernails (cutting): Fights with best friends
Fingernails (short): Misunderstanding will be patched
Fingernails (very long): Greed and thoughtlessness
Flesh (boils on): Scandals to soon hit
Flesh (decrease): Money loss and lack of love
Flesh (increase): Prosperity comes in strange ways
Flesh (scalding): Temper tantrum to cause heartache
Flesh (sores on): Theft or other dishonesty
Flesh (yellow): Sickness and disease may cause problems
Forehead (large): Success in business or profession
Forehead (narrow): Intelligent actions will be lacking
Forehead (small): Losses through stupidity
Hair (all over body): Dishonor and disgrace
Hair (beautiful): Outstanding luck in all things

Hair (combing): Frustrations to be worked out
Hair (cutting): Expect a loss of love through stupidity
Hair (thin or falling): Total failure in new endeavor
Hair (turning gray): Sickness and other bad things
Hair (turning white): Stunning news
Hands (beautiful and strong): Happiness in love and work
Hands (extra): Success in business. Happiness in love
Hands (injured or cut off): Loss of job, general failure
Hands (withered): Mental unrest and obstacles
Head (cut off or injured): Expect someone to try and ruin you
Head (extra): Good health and much money
Head (ill-formed): Very little success foreseen
Head (well-formed): Many honors, success to come
Head (with horns): New distinctions will soon develop
Intestines: Severe sickness, money problems not easily solved
Knees: Rewards for working hard
Knees (broken): Loss of job, loss of love
Knees (cut or bleeding): Business problems
Legs (fine condition): Many new and exciting adventures
Legs (lame): Stupidity can cause losses
Legs (scrawny): Failure caused by laziness
Lips (full and red): Gain of attention
Lips (withered): Little respect from others
Liver: Fun ruined through undeserved criticism
Mouth (bad taste in): Contempt from close associates
Mouth (dumb): Expect some serious sickness
Mouth (firmly closed): Something told in confidence
Mouth (large): Expect to gain in many areas
Mouth (small): Selfishness to rule actions
Muscles (shrunken): A multitude of failures
Muscles (well-developed): Successes in almost everything
Mustache: Degrading acts ruled by vain thoughts
Mustache (on woman): A warning to be discreet in activities
Mustache (shaved): Opportunity to make amends
Neck (broken): Bad luck befalls dreamer
Neck (severed): Untimely death or other disaster
Neck (strong): Much achievement and character strength
Neck (swollen): Illness forthcoming

Neck (twisted): Disgrace and dishonor
Neck (withered): Misery and possible illness
Nose (bleeding): Humiliation and shame
Nose (blowing): Annoyances to disappear
Nose (extra): Meddling people create troubles
Nose (large): Great honors for little achievement
Nose (none): An immoral act to cause distress
Nose (small): Success will be restrained
Ribs: Sadness and total lack of funds
Ribs (broken): Lover to leave unexpectedly
Ribs (losing): Expect a divorce or separation
Shoulders (injured): Family problems insurmountable
Shoulders (weak): A change of heart may hurt
Shoulders (well-developed): Plan on moving up in the world
Side (healthy): Business success and new loves
Side (wounded): Sorrow to engulf those around you
Skeleton: An enemy causes harm
Skull: A warning to be careful in activities
Teeth (decayed): Money losses and possible poverty
Teeth (extra): Relatives to be fighting
Teeth (losing): Lover to depart, friends to deceive
Teeth (white): Prosperity to come with happiness
Thigh (strong): Many successful trips for fun and business
Thigh (withered): Obstacles temporarily halt success
Thigh (wounded): Sickness while traveling
Tongue: Gossip causes bitterness with friends
Ugly: A multitude of misfortunes
Vaccination: Mental anguish to create discomfort
Veins (bleeding): Terrible illness to strike
Veins (normal): Good health. Cease to fret
Veins (swollen): Sadness and anxiety over trite things
Wounded: Sorrow created by severe mental anguish

CHAPTER 12

Human Actions

And Solomon awoke; and, behold, it was a dream.
1. Kings, 3:15

Feelings and physical activities expressed in a dream are relatively important in uncovering the true meaning of the entire dream. When a dream appears to be perfect and is indicative of good luck, yet there is a feeling of fear or fretfulness, it means that some hidden peril is lurking close at hand. The things we see in a dream that are tied to the sensations experienced or actions taken, sometimes give clues to distress or disappointment. Such problems may possibly be avoided.

Hymera, a woman of Syracuse, dreamed she was being carried to heaven by a strange young man. She looked around and was able to see the Gods of Olympus sitting on their thrones. A huge man with freckles and red hair was chained to the judgment throne of Jupiter. Hymera asked her youthful guide about the imprisoned man. He was said to be the "evil genius of Italy and Sicily." When his chains were finally broken, he would be responsible for the loss of many cities.

Upon awakening the next morning, Hymera told everyone of her unusual dream. Shortly thereafter, Dionysius, the tyrant, forcibly took the throne of Sicily. He marched into Syracuse where he was seen by Hymera. She revealed to all who would listen that Dionysius was the very same person she had seen chained during her dream. And Dionysius, learning of the tale, and fearing that Hymera might cause problems, ordered her put to death.

When physical activities in a dream appear to be difficult, impending sickness is foretold. Or success may be deterred by some insurmountable obstacle. Causing others to suffer in a dream, or making anyone feel humiliated, presages someone who is heartless coming into the dreamer's life. This visitor will try to harm the dreamer, and must be avoided.

Sounds which are heard in a dream are portents of danger. The dreamer should take precautions. Feelings of joyousness, when disturbing the continuity of the dream, are indicative of a forthcoming problem.

"A dream of Julius Caesar's of sexual relations with his mother has been handed down to us," declares Otto Rank, "which the oneiroscopists interpreted as a favourable omen signifying his taking possession of the earth."

Abandon: Neglectful friends cause sorrow
Abandon (by others): Some sorrow blended with relief
Abuse: Failure brought on by domineering attitude
Abuse (by others): Much ability but little faith in them
Accept: Success is doubtful for the present time
Accuse: Quarrels as a result of jealousy and suspicion
Acquit: Misunderstandings will quickly be resolved
Acquit (another): A friend will receive dreamer's generosity
Act (amateur): Humorous experiences to come soon
Act (circus): Foolish conduct will cause harm

Act (clown): Much entertaining of notables
Act (comedy): Chances harmed by ridiculous behavior
Act (professional): Few rewards for working diligently
Act (tragedy): Expect much sorrow and grief
Add: *See* Figure
Adopt: A warning to move, change residences
Aid: Advancement through good deeds
Aid (by others): Influential people will assist
Arrest: A warning to exert more caution
Arrest (of others): Assaults of enemy can easily be stopped
Awake: A new vision of life, wonderful tidings
Awake (others): Occasion to warn a friend, be on guard
Bathe (clear water): Happiness in everything
Bathe (muddy water): Sorrow and disgrace, dishonor
Bathe (running water): Contentment with pleasures of the flesh
Bathe (*See* others): Trouble caused by mental attitudes
Bathe (still water): New pleasures bring excitement
Bathe (water too hot): Anger makes burdensome problems
Bathe (with others): Undue familiarity with a stranger
Beat (a child or animal): Cruelty recoils back to self
Beat (by another person): Danger of being ruled by others
Beat (one your own size): Rivalry in love affairs
Beat (one bigger than yourself): Victory over great odds
Behead: Overwhelmed by those in positions of power
Behead (others): Opposition from unexpected source
Behead (*See* others): Great suffering due to ignorance
Blow (bubbles): Expectations vanish into thin air
Blow (nose): Relief from petty problems and vexations
Blow (on fire): Efforts will improve all affairs
Blow (out flame): Extinguishing happiness, little luck
Boast: Pride will depart with little warning
Borrow (book): Dependent on others for information
Borrow (others do it): Loss of friends and property
Borrow (umbrella or money): Loss of a dear friend
Break (chain of gold): Loss of relative
Break (chain of iron): Escape from limitations, new goals
Break (glass): All plans to fail due to inexperience
Break (urn): Never give up hope

Brush (clothes): Expect to be relieved from worry
Brush hair (easily): Pleasures and sensuality coming
Brush hair (with difficulty): Difficult problems and irritations
Burn (fields or woods): Indiscretion causes embarrassment
Burn (garbage): Avoidance of mental anguish
Buy: Gain in money and material things
Buy (another person): Problems arrive with success
Catch (birds or animals): Conquest of antagonists
Catch (in trap): New love and lust entanglements
Catch (others): Beware of trap, others seek to harm you
Chew (gum): Little success after much effort
Chew (tobacco): Watch for enemies who seem to be friends
Chew (tough meat): Overcoming all problems through diligence
Chew (tender meat): Good luck in all endeavors
Chop (wood): Success comes only against adversity
Climb (falling): Little accomplishment due to inability
Climb (falling after): Persistence pays after struggle
Climb (reach top): More effort will guarantee success
Climb (something unusual): New job brings financial gain
Confess (no forgiveness): Make amends or suffer consequences
Confess (receiving forgiveness): Close call from stupidity
Copy: Others allow you to depend upon them
Crawl (like an animal): Sensuality brings dishonor
Crawl (through tunnel): Little success in anything
Cry: Courage overcomes limitations
Cry (others): Sadness caused by others' problems
Curse: Discourtesy creates ire in associates
Dance (joyously): A new love and possible friendship
Dance (minuet): Social gain and financial worry
Dance (vulgarly): Lack of discretion creates trouble
Dance (waltz): A bliss-filled wedding
Die: Change of mind will bring better tidings
Die (for others): Difficult times in close proximity
Die (others in agony): Lack of selfishness to win over all
Dig (ditch): Creating insurmountable problems
Dig (grave): Never give up hope, things to change
Discharge (from job if happy): Expect better opportunity

Discharge (from job if sad): Unhappy situation not changing
Discharge (someone else): Troublemaker to go separate way
Dive (clear water): Doubtful success in chosen venture
Dive (muddy water): Dire danger and distress
Dream: Bliss in all things undertaken
Drive (horse): Financial gain and rise in status
Drive (others): A raise and a promotion
Drive (with difficulty): All bad things conquered
Drown: Great losses in every area of life, a warning
Drown (if rescued): Someone will offer help in time of need
Drown (others): Protection from cruel foes
Dye (hair or cloth): A drastic reversal in fortune
Eloping: Unfaithful lovers and unhappy marriage
Embracing (happily): A blissful marriage and new lover
Embracing (in sorrow): Many fights and misunderstandings
Embroidery: A good marriage with few problems
Embroidery (soiled): Happiness reversed by close friend
Escape: Overcome all obstacles and mental pressures
Escape (failing): New endeavors will surely fail
Fall (from chair): Loss of loved one to bitter enemy
Fall (into clear water): A drastic change for the better
Fall (into muddy water): Reputation marred by associates
Fall (regained footing): Will defeat all rivals
Fear: Expect some unfortunate thing to take place
Fear (very little): Many pleasures forthcoming
Fight (if overcome): Defeat by someone who wants to hurt you
Fight (winning): All things turn out for the best
Fight (to see others): Friends and associates will stand by you
Fight (with others): Business problems and fight with lover
Figures (adding): Financial gain and marriage of means
Figures (subtracting): Waste of money creates tension
Figures (multiplying): Many children and much more money
Figures (dividing): Good luck in almost all endeavors
Fish: Fun but little status and financial change
Follow (and overtake person): Everything successful
Follow (anyone escaping): Expect to fail in new things
Forge (chain): Friends to join together for happiness
Forge (horseshoe): Best of luck in everything

Forge (other things): Take advantage of better opportunities
Fly (in air alone): A new experience in the psychic realm
Fly (kite): Little results for difficult attempt
Gamble: Dishonor and sadness caused by dishonesty, beware of false friends and untrustworthy associates
Gather: Wealth is yours with little effort
Give (assistance): Rewards received for being nice
Give (gift): Others will misunderstand your objectives
Gossip: Problems created by thoughtless words, women should be on guard against flirtatious males
Harvest (plentiful): Business successes and luck in love
Harvest (scanty): Little reward for difficult labors
Harvest (shown by others): Expect to inherit a great deal of money
Hearing (a call): Offer help to a friend in need
Hearing (baying dogs): A warning of a death in the family
Hearing (birds): Nothing but bliss in the future
Hearing (chimes): A letter or a call from far away
Hearing (cock crowing): Boastful friend will create trouble
Hearing (cries): Sadness and mental anguish
Hearing (crows): Many problems to come
Hearing (donkey braying): Expect to inherit some cash
Hearing (echo): Friends try to deceive you
Hearing (groans): Stress and worry soon to pass
Hearing (hen cackling): Money gain and material comforts
Hearing (horse's neighing): Associates who are in powerful places
Hearing (hymns): Wedded bliss and happiness in other areas
Hearing (mocking laughter): Obstacles in way of plans
Hearing (music): *See* Chapter 18, Musical Instruments
Hearing (noises): Drastic reversals at home and in business
Hearing (owl hooting): Bad tidings and serious dangers
Hearing (shooting): Little marital bliss, loss of lover
Hearing (singing): Much happiness if singing is pretty
Hearing (stammering): Friend will try to deceive you
Hearing (steps): Be on guard against cruelty
Hearing (talking): Gossip by those who are supposed friends
Hearing (voice): Anguish over love, danger close at hand

Hide (from others): Cowardly acts never help in time of need
Hide (others hiding): Business matters are at a danger point
Hide (valuables): Friend will be hurt in climb to the top
Hunt (by others): Problems overcome by changing mind
Hunt (domestic animals): Greed will harm chances
Hunt (man): Little success in pursuit for money
Hunt (wild animals): Opposition defeated by strong will
Invite (by others): Pleasure ceases in relationship
Invite (guest): Bad decisions destroyed by insensitivity
Invite (stranger): Be careful who you spend time with
Iron (happily): Happiness at home and in business dealings
Iron (sticking): Problems and trouble to avoid if possible
Iron (cold): Loved ones give no affection for time being
Iron (hot): Passion overrides common sense
Jump (over things): Obstructions beaten through perserverance
Jump (rope): Laziness contributes to losses
Kill (animals): Family members and friends not dependable
Kill (ferocious beasts): Overcoming all opposition
Kill (others): Trouble caused by person seeking revenge
Kiss (enemy): Make amends with your friend
Kiss (family member): Nothing but bliss in all relationships
Kiss (mate): Lover ceases caring. Thoughtless actions
Kiss (sweetheart in dark): Undignified feelings in abundance
Kiss (sweetheart in light): A faithful sweetheart
Kiss (stranger): Scandalous life results in disgrace
Knit: Interference with stability at home
Laugh: Much laughter and bliss in all things
Laugh (uproariously): Regret felt because of ridiculous actions
Leave (friend): Little self-esteem and no lasting friends
Leave (home): Expect a change in many areas of life
Leave (mate): A warning of possible death or loss of love
Leave (position): New endeavors foreseen
Lend (anything): Friends will have change of mind
Lie: Beware of lying and cheating associates
Lie (others): Expect to be taken advantage of in business
Lose (clothing): Secret exposed by unexpected person
Lose (mate): Selfish actions cause despair
Lose (shoes): Someone out to get your job

Lose (sweetheart): Beware of competition in love life
Lose (valuables): Lack of caution can be devastating
Love (demonstrating): To meet someone new and marvelous
Love (happy on lover's lap): New love brings bliss
Love (indifferent): A lonely existence and few friends
Love (uneasy on lover's lap): Expect to feel distressed
Love (returned): Good news from someone you care for
Making (beds): A birth and unexpected visitors at home
Making (new material): Pleasant surroundings and people
Making (old material): Dire need for understanding
Making (pastry): Deception expected from old friend
Making (soap): Be content with what you now have
Making (will): Possible disaster in business enterprises
March (to march music): Time will be donated for good cause
March (others): News of associate will hurt you
Marry (foreigner): No travel in near future, little money
Marry (mate marry lover): Lover finds someone else
Marry (old man or woman): To wed for great deal of cash
Marry (remarry mate): Sympathetic feelings may cause problems
Marry (stranger): Sudden changes in all areas of life
Marry (sweetheart): Take on all new opportunities
Paint (anything): Changes in luck for the better
Pay (bills): Trust no one with your finances
Pay (by others): Expect to receive an old bill
Pay (dues): Good friends are ready to help
Pay (penalty): Forget past mistakes and try to do better
Pay (taxes): Honesty brings everything good
Pay (wages): Everyone offers friendship and aid
Photograph: Avoid deceit by being more careful
Photograph (by others): A supposed friend will try to deceive
Plan (business): Be cautious when entering new business
Plan (home): Expect a baby if married; a wedding for single dreamers; disaster for married lovers
Play (baseball): New friends and nice associates
Play (basketball): Friends will offer help
Play (billiards): Associates may try to take advantage
Play (cards): Good luck when gambling

Play (checkers): Serious doubt as to potential successes
Play (chess): Depressed feelings cause bad times
Play (dice): Little good luck when gambling
Play (games for fun): Better health and lack of home life
Play (games for kids): Friends lose respect over nothing
Play (golf): Gain of help from influential person
Play (marbles): Old friendship reestablished in time
Play (ninepins): Jaded friends take advantage when necessary
Play (quoits): Little progress towards success
Play (sports for fun): New friends and lovers add much to life
Play (tennis): Bliss in new love situation
Play music (accompaniment): Marriage in near future
Play music (drum): Marriage to someone in the military
Play music (duet): Bliss for those married who have lovers
Play music (in orchestra): Anguish over heartbreak
Play music (wind instrument): Destined to wed a musician
Polish: All conditions in life on the upswing
Pray (alone): Understanding by friends and lovers
Pray (unhappily): Sadness brought about through lack of tact
Preach: Strife created by busybodies who interfere
Preach (from pulpit): Much wisdom offered to assist others
Preach (others): Habits must be revised in order to gain
Punish (animals): Monetary gain ruined by cruelty
Punish (children): An unfortunate sign; beware of trouble
Punish (self): Mistakes bring on meddlers and problems
Quarrel: Criticism of honor and esteem
Quarrel (others): Good business relationship and happiness
Quarrel (with friends): Unkind acts court disaster
Race: Expect more competition before winning
Race (boat upsetting): A warning of danger; be careful
Race (failing): Little effort exerted towards success
Race (horses): A mixture of good luck and misfortune
Race (successful): Strength of character to defeat rivals
Read (bible): Understanding brings close associations
Read (fretfully): An unexciting life and little pleasure
Read (happily): Peace of mind and contentment with self
Read (history): Past experience will help carry you through tribulation

Read (romance): A new affair of the heart and financial gain
Read (with difficulty): Adverse conditions to overcome
Reap: *See* Harvest
Register (by assumed name): Discreet behavior pays well
Register (by another name): Others to take advantage of good nature
Register (own name): New attempts to do good will succeed
Rent (failing to rent): Try harder to reach goals
Rent (paying rent): Give up those things not needed
Rent (success in renting): Pleasure-filled evenings
Resign (against will): Expect a drastic change in fortune
Resign (with relief): Problems to be overcome immediately
Ride (forced to dismount): Some failure in best of plans
Ride (successfully): Distinction gained through heroic deed
Ride (thrown from horse): Friends to leave because of mistrust
Ride (while screaming): Beneficial changes in luck
Run: Competition is stiff in all areas of success
Run (falling down): Many plans will eventually fail
Run (slipping): Serious physical infirmity affects decisions
Run (stumbling): Take care when initiating anything new
Sail (rough water): Expect many difficulties
Sail (smooth water): Progress will be quick and trouble-free
Sail (stormy seas): Be on guard against impending danger
Save (by others): Appreciative associates will help
Save (food): Loss of friendship through neglect
Save (life): Many rewards for good deeds and kindness
Save (money): Lovers will never cease caring
Seek (hidden money or treasure): Scheming friend is a problem
Seek (shelter): Look for refuge with a friend
Seek (underground cave): Care required for ultimate safety
Sell (to advantage): A new love and a fast start in business
Sell (to disadvantage): Ruination may take place through deceit
Sew (basting): Secret adversary can create trouble
Sew (buttons): Prosperity staring you in the face
Sew (mending clean clothing): Monetary gain and good luck
Sew (mending filthy clothing): Surprising changes for the good
Sew (patching): Help will arrive when needed most
Sew (something new): Unexpected pleasures and much fun

Shave (easily): Life will go along smoothly
Shave (by others): Others will try to strongly influence you
Shave (with difficulty): Obstacles in pathway to success
Shake hands (with distaste): A new enemy will be encountered
Shake hands (with pleasure): A new friend will be met
Sharpen (instrument): Response to danger must be quick
Sharpen (tool): Action required to avoid desperate situation
Sharpen (knife): Avoid any contact with business associates
Sing (at funeral): Loved one may soon pass away
Sing (duet): Soon to find bliss in lovemate
Sing (hymns): Good thoughts encompass every moment
Sing (in tune): Everything goes smoothly for lovers
Sing (out of tune): Expect no cooperation from friends
Sing (quartette): Many friends to suggest bad things
Sing (serenade): Give more time to your lovers
Skate (on ice): Practice more cautious moves
Skate (on sidewalk): Flirting may bring disaster
Sleep (alone): Avoid too many relationships for now
Sleep (with a child): Peace of mind comes slowly
Sleep (with a stranger): Many bad experiences to be avoided
Sleep (with an animal): Disgrace and scandal created by activities
Sleep (with lover): Beware of the opposite sex
Sleep (with mate): Few troubles are insurmountable
Slide (over grass): Many will try to deceive for money
Slide (over snow): Happy times with close friends
Slide (upsetting while sliding): Avoid critical people
Slide (upsetting while steering): Serious problems to erupt
Smell (a rose): A fine marriage and plenty of everything
Smell (disgusting): Associates will try to cause disharmony
Smell (wonderful): A great change for the better
Smoke (cigar): Luxury abounds with little happiness
Smoke (cigarette): Lack of seriousness will bring evil
Smoke (pipe): Many nice things at home to happen soon
Sow (in good soil): Much luck in all endeavors
Sow (in poor soil): Miscalculations are reasons to fail
Spit (on someone): Good times to abruptly cease
Spit (on by others): Few people give any respect for actions

Steal: Failure through jealousy and greed
Steal (money): Bad decisions regarding finances
Steal (spoons): Home life marred by pitiful acts
Steal (by others): Be on guard against competitors
Step: *See* Tread
Strike (a child): Take advantage of every situation
Strike (an animal): Dishonor and disgrace through thoughtlessness
Strike (a man): Mental anguish and fighting between friends
Strike (a woman): Taking advantage of friends breeds ill-will
Struggle: Sickness to result from stress and worry
Struggle (by others): Help the person who requests aid
Study: Much planning necessary to succeed
Study (by others): Someone trying to outdo you in everything
Swear: *See* Curse
Swim (easily): Everything will meet with ultimate success
Swim (under water): Others meet secretly to destroy you
Swim (with difficulty): All opponents defeated with effort
Talk: Unthinking words reflect lack of forethought
Talk (by others): Personal life comes under attack
Tease: Selfishness creates disharmony
Teased by others: An enemy to try to disrupt everything
Travel (if crowded): Friends turn into competitors
Travel (in luxury): Many happy tidings and good deeds
Tread (on by others): Take a stand for principles
Tread (on others): Enemies created by brutish actions
Tread (on snake): Winning foreseen in all endeavors
Visit (blissful): Pleasant surroundings and nice experiences
Visit (sad): Spiteful attitude brings humiliating gesture
Vow: Promises will not be kept in good fath
Walk (on railroad rails): A new and exciting venture
Walk (on railroad ties): A reversal of good luck temporarily
Walk (on walls): Little security but much hope
Walk (in pleasant places): Prospects are better than ever
Walk (in dangerous places): Beware of changing partners
Wash clothes (in brook): All things to improve in time
Wash clothes (in muddy water): Scandal causes vexation
Wash clothes (in ocean): Controversy over activities

Weave: All attempts to succeed are wasted at this time
Weed: Problem areas can be bettered by trying harder
Weep: Lovers will come to grips with serious problems
Work (with distaste): Sickness as a result of stress and agony
Work (with pleasure): Job will pay better than expected
Write (to enemy): Practice more caution when speaking
Write (to friend): Be honest in dealing with others
Write (to loved one): Learn your limitations
Write (to lover): Say nothing you'll later regret
Yelling: Some illness is foreseen. Inactive love life

CHAPTER 13

Food and Drink

We all dream; we do not understand our dreams, yet we act as if nothing strange goes on in our sleep minds. . . .

Eric Fromm

Physical sensations obtained while eating or drinking are important in the proper interpretation of a dream. How the food is served, how tasty or repulsive it looks, whether it is fresh or stale—all of these things give clues that help in arriving at accurate interpretations.

Monetary gain and sensual pleasures are indicated by dreaming of any food that tastes delicious. Bad tasting food presages humiliation and dishonor. The omen is even worse if the food is seen smeared on the face, lips, and hands of the dreamer. Any bitter-tasting food denotes an experience usually filled with unpleasantness. But the end result will be good for the dreamer. Greasy food portends the same thing.

Food with no seasoning and rather tasteless food always portend displeasure with the dreamer's surroundings. This can be readily changed for the better, with a little forethought and effort on the part of the dreamer.

Raw foods such as apples, oranges, celery, cucumbers, pineapple, and so on, are explained in Chapters 3 and 7.

Any food denoting something good in its interpretation, yet nauseating in a dream, reveals deceit by someone from whom the dreamer least expects it. If a food carrying an unfavorable connotation pleases the dreamer, it indicates that the dreamer is subject to fraud.

Gluttonous eating shows greed that will cause friends to avoid the dreamer. Opportunities will be few and far between. Heavy drinking symbolizes impending physical ailments, and possible problems in all areas of life. Eating alone in a dream signifies that marriage is not a good idea. Quietly sharing a meal with someone else presages a possible marriage filled with happiness or a wonderful love affair. But, if your meal companion is mannerless, or argumentative, expect to be taken advantage of by false friends and coveting associates.

Preparing food to cook or bake is not as favorable a sign as is eating. Anxiety and frustration are presaged, however favorably the food omen is interpreted. Food in abundance signifies never doing without life's important needs. Food in short supply indicates a substantial lack of material goods and wealth.

"It would seem then, after all, that dreams are not the utter nonsense they have been said to be by such authorities as Chaucer, Shakespeare, and Milton," offers J. Sully. "The chaotic aggregations of our night-fancy have a significance and communicate new knowledge."

Bacon (cutting): Enemies will be defeated
Bacon (rancid): Problems and disagreeable situations
Bacon (raw): Danger lurks at every turn
Bacon (sweet and fresh): Expect success in everything
Beef (fatty): Arguments from closest friends
Beef (raw): Much danger of physical abuse
Beef (well-cooked): Relaxation and comfort through life
Beer (bitter): A change of luck for the better
Beer (cold): Lacking finances even with hard work
Beer (frothy): Unexpected problems may arise
Beer (hot): Affection from an unexpected source

Beer (smooth): Trouble in love and marriage
Biscuits: An argumentive spouse or friend
Brandy: Actions will drive away companions
Bread (brown): Best of health
Bread (graham): Health will soon improve
Bread (moldy): Quarrels
Bread (sour): Distress
Bread (wheat): Improvement in financial standing
Bread (white): Riches soon coming
Breakfast (appetizing): A very lucky day
Breakfast (distasteful): Bad luck in all things
Broth: True friendship will aid you, an enduring attachment
Butter: Hard work brings wealth and success
Buttermilk: Little foresight brings on sadness
Cakes (plain): Expect to meet a hospitable partner
Cakes (rich): New endeavors will prove to be fun
Cakes (wedding, another's): A wedding soon coming
Cakes (wedding, your own): Disappointment in love matters
Candy: Ardent lovemaking in near future
Cheese (cream): Riches
Cheese (moldy): Friends will leave because of attitudes
Cheese (rich): Material wealth to be given you
Cheese (strong): Disgrace and humiliation
Chocolate: Extremely good health and best of luck
Cider (hard): Many problems and much strife
Cider (sweet): An honest lover will enter your life
Coffee: Marriage will be fought by friends
Cornmeal: Success in business and other affairs
Cream: Much pleasure and plenty of affluence
Custard: A new experience may prove revolting
Dessert: Surprises in the sensual realm of life
Dinner (plentiful): Abundance of everything
Dinner (scarcity): Hard times coming
Eggs: Unhappiness abounds for the time being
Eggs (yolk broken): Troubles
Flour: Peace of mind and bliss at home and business
Gin: irritation created by unexpected problems
Gravy (clear): Many problems are overcome before succeeding

Gravy (greasy): Friends will mislead you in every manner
Grease: Undertakings meet with complete success
Grease (smeared with): A friend chooses to disagree firmly
Ham: All things will turn out well
Hominy: Expect to not be without anything
Honey: Success through positive thinking
Honey (very fresh): Realization of hopes for lovers
Ice cream: Prominent associates offer soap and water
Ice cream soda: All friends and lovers are pleased
Jam: Much wealth and many nice things
Jelly: Old associates will not forget during times of need
Lard (rancid): Scandalous activities breed disruption
Lard (sweet): A rise in the world of business
Lemonade: Ill friends and family members will recover; enemies will not survive sickness
Lunch (basket): Jolly outing in store for you
Lunch (formal): Social rise coming very soon
Macaroni: Greed brings unexpected trouble
Meat (beef): A comfortable life in store for you
Meat (lamb): Material goods not lacking in home
Meat (pork): Try to overcome all problems
Meat (stew): Bad fortune blended with good fortune
Milk: Health and excellent fortune
Molasses: Entanglement in love or business affairs
Mustard: Too much careless conversation
Nutmeg: A trip to a new place brings happiness
Oatmeal: Prime health is foreseen as is much success
Oil (rancid): Friend to humiliate you unexpectedly
Oil (sweet): Lovers and friends to make up shortly
Pancakes: Irritations will bring about defeat
Pastry: Petty fights and much dishonesty
Pepper: Spiteful person will make you angry
Pickles: An experience mingled with sorrow and joy
Pies: Attempted deception. Beware of flirtations
Poultry: Expect to be harried over small minds
Poultry (cleaning): Do what must be done, whatever the cost
Puddings: Guests to drop in without invitation, problems caused for married couples

Punch: Expect some friends to change loyalties
Raisins: Disappointment reigns in spite of tact
Salad (fruit): Much exciting entertainment
Salad (vegetable): Problems with health due to pressures
Salt: Living conditions bettered through good thoughts
Salt (spilled): Family members will constantly bicker
Sausage: A multitude of goodness but some vexations
Soda: Take advantage of this new opportunity
Soup (burned): Fighting brings on more problems
Soup (clear broth): Contentment in everything
Soup (creamy): Money to soon arrive unexpectedly
Sugar: Success stopped by adverse deeds, avoid jealousy
Sugar (in bowl): Try to stop enemies before they are done
Supper: Someone in the family to have a child
Tea: Gossip creates much strife and unhappiness
Venison: Changes and reversals in everything
Vinegar: Illness and fighting among associates
Water (clear): Anxiety will cause heartbreak
Water (cool): Little peace for those who curse
Water (hot): Rash actions bring on problems
Water (tepid): Grave misfortune and insurmountable problems
Whiskey: Money losses and sadness over loved one's actions
Wine: Play the game honestly to retain friends
Wine (too much): Unavoidable errors seem to entertain others
Yeast: No bad sickness. Conditions to get better

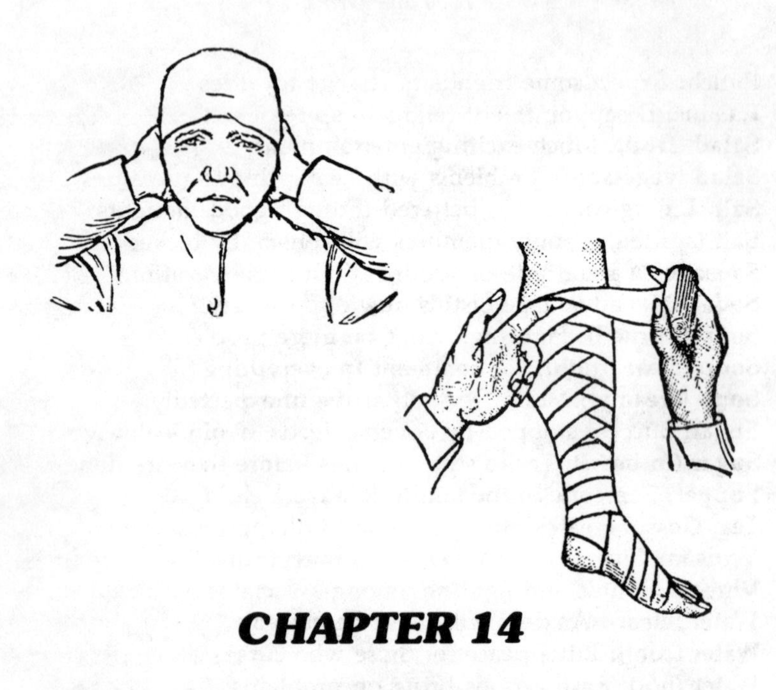

CHAPTER 14

Illness and Medicines

And it shall come to pass in the last days, saith God . . . your old men shall dream dreams:

Acts, 2:17

Dreams of a chill or a fever may result from too little or too many blankets on a bed. Such dreams should not be taken seriously, unless the reasons are otherwise. Dreaming of a throat or lung infection, a toothache, sore joint, or any feelings of severe pain, are all presages of impending sickness. Such illnesses can usually be averted if the dreamer takes proper precautions.

Any head injury or mental problem erupting in a dream simply denotes unnecessary worry or too much mental strain. Stomach pain or nausea warn the dreamer of indigestion, or of the danger of being poisoned by an enemy. Nervousness and stress are foreseen when one dreams of measles or any other similar skin irritation. The dreamer is being warned to relax more often and slow down in lifestyle. More time should be spent undertaking out-of-doors activities. Fatigue or weakness felt in a dream portends a change of career is probable in the near future.

"If only it were always possible to interpret dreams correctly," muses Lynkus. "That is certainly not an easy task, but with a little attention it must always be possible to the dreamer."

Dreaming of a laxative denotes that all anxiety will soon disappear. All other problems will soon be forgotten. Dreaming of ointments used for soothing the body represents consolation after being degraded, or following much sadness.

St. Augustine tells how Gennadius, a physician from Carthage, was thoroughly convinced of the soul's immortality after conversing with an apparition of a young man in one of his many dreams. Gennadius was firmly told: "As you can see when your bodily eyes are closed in sleep, so you will find that when your bodily senses are extinct in death, you will see and hear with the sense of your spirit."

Abscess: Sensual desires bring about troubles
Aches: Bad times in business and love matters
Birth (for married women): Great rejoicing, many good things
Birth (unmarried girl): Disgrace and unhappiness, a bad omen
Birth (twins or triplets): Success in the most difficult things
Birth (seeing an eagle born): Future greatness for child
Birth (seeing a fish born): Sensitivity and kindness
Birth (seeing an unfavorable symbol born): A dire warning
Bleeding: Losses and danger
Bleeding (nose): Beware of an angry person
Boils: Vexations will be caused by friends and relatives
Bronchitis: Guard against seemingly good friends
Burns: A sign of a coming fever
Calomel: Expect problems to disappear, contentment
Cancer: Great trouble and sorrow
Canker: Criticism from all sides will cause harm
Castor oil: Problems will be overcome in short time period

Chilblains: Others with influence cause unnecessary trouble
Chills: A slight illness is unavoidable
Cholera: Disease may strike, be careful in all dealings
Cold: Be alert against health hazards, anxiety over friends
Consumption: Sickness can cause heartache, be cautious
Cough: Be wary of dangerous situations and friends
Disease: No need to fret over stability and health
Dizziness: *See* Vertigo
Dropsy: Difficulties will be short-lived, expect changes
Fainting: Bad tidings, nothing good in near future
Fatigue: Don't worry about things, goodness brings chaos
Feebleness: Stand firm for your beliefs, a fine letter to come
Fever: Much mental stress over lost friendships
Fit: Exciting times ahead. Always practice honesty
Fluctuating illness: Grave situation will turn out for the best
Gangrene: A scandal results from illicit actions
Gout: Greedy people surround you at present
Herbs: *See* Chapter 7
Hives: Pressures cause mental unbalance in associate
Hydrophobia: Anger breeds more trouble. Be wary of everyone
Indigestion: Someone is trying to cause disruptions
Infirmities: *See* Chapter 11
Insanity: Leave troubles behind, look ahead more positively
Itch: Emotional problems mount steadily for lovers
Jaundice: Prospects are presently discouraging
Leprosy: Thievery and lies bring undeserved money
Madness: *See* Insanity
Measles: Much anxiety over lost love and broken friendship
Numbness: *See* Paralysis
Ointment: Constant distress will change to happiness
Pain: Illness will be short-lived, monetary gain
Palsy: Present situation to quickly change for the best
Paralysis: Be on guard against those who would do you in
Pills: Bad luck and serious consequences for those who wait
Poison: Everything looks terrible but will change in time
Pulse (taking own): Give more attention to loved ones
Pulse (taking someone else's): Alert others to evil influences
Quinine: Health will get better, try to be patient in love

Rheumatism: Expect better things in the future
Ringworm: Experiences will prove beneficial soon
Rupture: Fighting among friends and lovers
Smallpox: Expect the unexpected, times are fast-changing
Suffocation: Dishonor comes as a result of frivolous acts
Tumor: All problems are defeated, keep an open mind
Urination: A disagreeable situation to come to a head
Vertigo: Mental confusion under outside pressures
Vomiting: Friends will try to disrupt for no good reason

CHAPTER 15

Ships and Related Items

For we have in the dream . . . sworn fealty to the wild, incalculable, creative forces, the Imagination of the Universe.

Isak Dinesen

Ships and boats of any kind signify some sort of business endeavor, love arrangement, or dangerous situation. A vessel's overall fitness is important in understanding the dream's full meaning. The weather condition at sea is also extremely important in a dream. Quiet seas and good sailing breezes connotate a happy marriage and favorable love life. A stormy sea indicates the opposite.

A disabled ship wallowing at sea portends impending danger. A ship in excellent running condition presages bliss in marriage and much luck in love situations. This is especially true if the object of the dreamer's affection is also present in the dream.

On Good Friday morning, April 14, 1865, President Abraham Lincoln was meeting with his cabinet. He opened the session with this statement: "Gentlemen, something very extraordinary is going to happen, and that very soon."

"Something good, sir, I hope," his Attorney General responded.

"I don't know, I don't know, but it *will* happen, and shortly, too."

"Have you received any information, sir," queried the Attorney General, "not yet disclosed to us?"

"No," the President answered gravely, "but I have had a dream; and I have now had the same dream three times—once on the night preceding the battle of Bull Run, once on a night preceding another battle not favorable to the North."

Lincoln and the others sat quietly reflecting on his words. His Attorney General again spoke up: "Might one ask the nature of the dream, sir?"

"Well," offered the President, "I am on a great, broad, rolling river, and I am in a boat, and I drift, and I drift—but this is not business!"

Lincoln suddenly stiffened, looked around the table, and changed the subject: "Let us proceed to business, gentlemen!"

Later, that very Friday night, Lincoln was assassinated.

Anchor: All hopes soon realized, smile always
Boat: Success in everything undertaken
Boat (falling out of): Disaster will strike soon
Boat (leaky): A new love will prove dangerous to happiness
Boat (old): An affair which should be abandoned immediately
Cabin: Endurance pays in the end, never quit
Canoe (if another paddles): Others will aid when required
Canoe (if paddling): Only you can make the future bright
Canoe (with man): Expect no help from friends
Canoe (with woman): Wedded bliss is on the way
Compass (whirling needle): Exciting things to take place
Compass (pointing north): Keep your nose to the grindstone
Compass (pointing south): A change in career is necessary

Deck: Little security in present frame of mind
Deck (slippery): Avoid dangerous problem with wits
Deck (steady in storm): All danger will quickly pass
Docks: Temporary distress. Fear no harm for now
Docks (difficulty in docking): Business problems foreseen
Docks (filled with cargo): Financial gain is certain
Ferry: Success depends upon your attitude, try harder
Fleet (good weather): New opportunities to succeed
Fleet (stormy weather): Avoid trouble with common sense
Gunboat: Fighting among mates and friends
Gunboat (many): Insurmountable troubles coming fast
Lifeboat: Stranger will help when needed most
Lighthouse (good weather): A good omen, luck surrounds you
Lighthouse (stormy weather): All difficulties will be turned away
Navy: Happiness and success in everything
Navy (run down ships): Gambling will prove costly
Oars: A new enterprise will surely succeed
Oars (broken): Stumbling blocks are in the way of success
Oars (one lost): Everything goes wrong on a temporary basis
Oars (rowing with difficulty): Unneeded responsibilities
Pier: Take a long trip for pleasure
Pier (much shipping): Trips will help financially
Quarantine: Little progress at work because of schemers
Raft (safe on one): Success doubtful for time being
Raft (sinking): Forsake all previous endeavors
Rubber boat: Despair in love matters and money losses
Ship (filled with cargo): Good luck in business
Ship (dawn sailing): Everything looking better by the day
Ship (sinking): Unexpected disaster in all areas of life
Ship (sinking with it): Unavoidable troubles, expect the worst
Ship (sunset sailing): Peaceful thoughts and much gain
Spyglass: New ideas will pay off handsomely
Spyglass (broken): Evildoers will disappear, luck to change
Steering gear: Friends offer everything for cash outlay
Submarine: Possible disaster in the making
Torpedo: Horrible experiences forthcoming

Warship: Disharmony in the home and with acquaintances
Warship (many): A brewing quarrel among closest friends
Wreck (at sea): A disaster to appear and drain of funds
Wreck (in sand): Temptations to go away, avoid close friends

CHAPTER 16

Buildings

The prophet that hath a dream, let him tell a dream . . .

Jeremiah, 23:28

A multitude of buildings seen in excellent condition portend good luck in business dealings and in all new endeavors. Everything undertaken will be eminently successful. However, if the dreamer sees a rundown building, success will not be soon forthcoming. If a building is seen in total ruins, failure in all endeavors cannot be avoided.

A prominent citizen of Lyons had a dream in which he was run over by a wild horse. He approached Kircher, a Jesuit, for an interpretation. He was assured that a horse would surely be the direct cause of his death. The man was terrified of horses from that day on and avoided them at every turn.

The gentleman had forgotten to tell Kircher the rest of his dream—that the trampling took place at a local pub. This was certainly the key to the danger presaged by the dream. The man went out during a storm and dropped by the local inn for a drink. Upon leaving, with the storm still raging, a sign was blown down. It struck him on the head and killed him instantaneously. The sign had been hanging over the door of the inn. And on it was painted a huge black horse!

Another instance of dreams relating to buildings comes from a very ancient source. When a king dreamed he was in his palace, and he saw a lioness and her cubs, it prophesied that the queen and his children would prove to be a source of great contentment.

Abbey: Troubles through serious lawsuits
Abbey (in ruins): Plans and aspirations will fail
Academy: Neglected studies will cause regret
Almshouse: Lack of many things, especially in a marriage
Apartment (attractive): Wedded bliss foreseen
Apartment (dreary): Happiness will be lost through idleness
Art gallery: Disharmony in love and business life
Bank: Business will prosper and allow early retirement
Barn (empty): Opportunity knocks for those who are prepared
Barn (full): Nothing lacking in material things you need
Barracks: Irritations and minor arguments with family
Boardinghouse: Upsetting situation will be short-lived
Castle: Much unexpected travel to gain lots of cash
Cathedral: An increase in money. Dignified meeting
Chapel: Mental peace and a friend who consoles when needed
Convent: Emotional turmoil can be expected
Cottage (pretty): A home filled with happiness and fun
Cottage (ruined): Annoyances will make you terribly upset
Dairy: Financial gain if cows are quiet and contented
Factory (busy): Expect to have many new chances to succeed
Factory (idle): Plans go wrong, many problems to overcome
Fort: Someone unexpectedly attacks, but fear nothing
Home (in disorder): Eruption of bad feelings
Home (neat and clean): Happiness in marriage

Hospital: Sickness will strike someone near and dear
Hotel: Gain of money comes slowly after traveling
House (building one): A drastic change for the better
House (custom-built): Obstacles will slow chances
House (dilapidated): Misery arrives in small doses
House (in ruins): Bad health and financial losses
House (new): Lovers will find ultimate bliss
House (tiny and poor): A warning to be more careful
Inn: Friends will stick by you under duress
Jail (entering): Practice more caution in all situations
Jail (leaving): Avoid dishonest activities or pay the price
Market (empty): Life is full of unfortunate things at present
Market (fish): Financial gain and change of luck
Market (flowers): Attention from unexpected quarter
Market (vegetables): Fights and problems in home life
Mill (busy): Everything turns out better with time
Mill (idle): Act now or lose the battle for health and love
Mill (in ruins): Some sort of drastic reversal to take place
Morgue: A letter or a call warning of a death
Observatory: Read carefully and success will be yours
Palace: Things change for the good if you are patient
Palace (in ruins): Beware of deceitful relatives and friends
Post office: A package from some foreign country
Prison: Little foresight causes unfortunate events
Prison (leaving): Problems are overcome quickly
School: A raise and a promotion are coming soon
School (when a child): Expect changes of luck for the worst
Shanty: Money will be difficult to get, hold tight
Shelter: Someone will offer a hand of friendship
Slaughterhouse: Sickness and terrible experience will hinder
Stable: Never gamble or you stand to lose all
Store: *See* Market
Store (china or antiques): Be cautious or suffer consequences
Store (drugs): A marvelous blend of ill luck and good luck
Store (dry goods): Everything appears positive for success
Store (empty): All plans go off course temporarily
Store (full): Financial gain can be seen in near future
Store (meat): Problems to overcome. Mental anguish

Theater: A lover will surprise you with something nice
Theater (*See* Comedy): Friends will try to make you smile
Theater (*See* Tragedy): Others try to make you feel guilt
Warehouse (empty): Deception leads to possible ruin
Warehouse (full): All endeavors successful in time
Warehouse (burning): Danger of losing investments
Warehouse (in ruins): Possible bankruptcy if not careful

CHAPTER 17

Contents of Buildings

Dreams are rudiments of the great state to come.
We dream what is about to happen.

Philip James Bailey

Neat and clean rooms are good omens when seen in a dream. So are nicely appointed furnishings when seen in a room. Messy rooms denote problems arising from laziness and self-centeredness. If a room is seen empty or sparsely furnished, it is a sign that things are lacking in the dreamer's life. Poverty is also a strong possibility. There is an exception to this rule.

When a destitute individual dreams of an empty room, it portends no immediate change in their financial status.

Clean furniture and other things found in a room or in a building indicates success and good luck. Rooms in disorder signify mental confusion and haphazard habits. Broken, soiled, or filthy furniture and other items suggest that problems and embarrassment will result from impulsiveness and evil thoughts. If the room is full of furniture it is generally taken as a good omen unless some of the items otherwise represent a negative sign. If a bad symbol is seen in a full room, it means that there will be obstructions to success. If the room of a building is leaking when it rains, there will be a financial loss and bad investments. Any object seen in a room that is accidently broken by the dreamer is a warning to be more cautious in order to gain success and good fortune.

Delavigne was a highly educated intellectual living in Dijon. He had labored for days over a passage in a Greek poem, and was unable to properly translate and understand the meaning of the words. He went to bed one night and had a dream of being transported to the palace of Queen Christina in Stockholm. He saw himself in what appeared to be a marvelous library, selected a small book, and began to read. The volume was Greek poetry and it contained the same passages he failed to understand while awake. Now they made sense and he was amazed at the ease with which he could translate. Delavigne awoke from his stupor and excitedly began to write down his translation.

Finding this revelation so extraordinary, he immediately wrote a letter to Descartes, who was then in Sweden as a member of the Queen's Court. He described everything in detail which had so uniquely taken place in his dream. Descartes, the great philosopher, was impressed. He responded that even the most skilled architect could not have supplied a more accurate description of the palace library and the books it contained. He had searched in the spot mentioned by Delavigne and found the exact volume of Greek poetry. He read the lines quoted and verified the accuracy of Delavigne's translation.

Descartes

Attic: Deception by others, little hope for good
Altar (in ruins): Make amends for past misdeeds
Altar (lighted): Expect spiritual gain
Altar (with flowers): Good fortune to arrive soon
Balcony: Avoid flirtations. A new lover to come
Bar: Success gained through deceit and lies
Basement: Sadness and ill-feelings influence decisions
Basin (empty): Unexpected danger, possible death
Basin (full): Expect to make money and gain status
Bed or bedding (clean): Problems shall go away
Bed or bedding (neat): Friends to help in time of need
Bed or bedding (dirty): Problems in love life
Bed or bedding (unmade): Problems with those at home
Blackboard (empty): Few obstacles to success
Blackboard (full): Hard work will bring gain in finances
Blotting paper: Write nothing to later regret
Boiler: Loss of finances and grave disappointment
Book (good condition): Money to be made while having fun
Book (soiled): Conditions create sad situation in business
Book (torn cover): Nothing seems to go well for the present

Book (torn pages): A serious mistake in judgment
Bottles (empty): Regret felt over what happened in the past
Bottles (full): A cheerful disposition brings better luck
Bottles (new): Things to get better if you persist
Bottles (old): Try something different for a change
Broom (new): Great financial changes are in store soon
Broom (old): Keep a wary eye on where your money goes
Bureau (disorderly): A mix-up causes unavoidable delays
Bureau (empty): Shortages of cash prove a hindrance
Bureau (full): Everything goes well for those who exert effort
Bureau (neat): Prosperity is foreseen coming shortly
Candle (bright): New love, little illness, and bliss
Candle (dim): A serious argument causes strain
Candle (new): Someone dear to you gives birth
Candle (snuffing out flame): Mistake in a decision brings sadness
Candle (wasting away): Mate to depart with close friend
Cellar: Illness and much sadness forthcoming
Chair (arm): Newfound status in business world
Chair (broken): A companion will deceive you
Chair (rocking): Household troubles if not careful
Chimney: Mind-boggling changes for the better
Chimney (smoking): A death in the family causes strife
China: Fretful times are on the way now
China (broken): Delicate situation needs solving with kindness
Clock: An enemy to strike when least expected
Clock (in tower): Be not fearful of danger, it will pass
Clock (stopping): Job will be lost but better one found
Clock (striking): Cease wasting time or lose everything
Coal hod: Mental disharmony causes a waste of effort
Cot: An offer of temporary employment to be refused
Corkscrew: Difficulties experienced in love life
Cradle: Meeting a new friend and possible mate
Crockery (abundant): No problems in the home arena
Crockery (broken): Fights and arguments with loved ones
Cupboard (empty): Bad tidings brought about through neglect
Cupboard (disorderly): Run and hide from coming trouble
Cupboard (well-filled): A change in luck for the better

Cupola: Something lost will be soon located
Curtains (dirty): Argumentive friend creates anguish
Curtains (fresh): Unwelcome visitor to cause a problem
Curtains (torn): Regretful actions are to be undertaken
Cushion: Business successes bring new problems
Desk (empty): Write nothing of any importance
Desk (piled high): Time to take care of unfinished business
Dome: Lucky things to happen right now
Elevator (going down): Expectations much too high
Elevator (going up): All plans will succeed despite problems
Forks: Rival is trying to get your job
Forks (bent): Experience problems in marriage or with lover
Furnace (bright fire): All endeavors to work out well
Furnace (no fire): Bitterness and hard feelings over choices
Furnace (woman attending): Laziness is reason for failure
Jug (empty): Little good foreseen, be on guard
Jug (full): The best of all things to soon happen
Jug (leaking): Good luck changes to bad unless careful
Keg (empty): Nothing is in the way of success
Keg (full): Woman to try and create problems for sweethearts
Keg (leaking): Offended by a close friend, unforgiving
Kettle: Rejoice because of a fortunate opportunity
Key (breaking): Little reward because of inexperience
Key (bright): Wealth is just around the corner, keep trying
Key (bunch): New opportunities lie ahead for alert people
Key (finding): Bliss and happiness in love matters
Key (losing): Friend to pull away and deceive you
Knife: Share your prosperity or pay the price
Lamp (clean): Bitter disappointments in all plans
Lamp (dirty): Laziness brings ruination unless changes are made
Lamp (with light on): Much ability seen to win over all odds
Lamp (with light off): Unkind deeds should be guarded against
Lantern (bright light): Folly causes regret
Lantern (lighting one): Hurt by a friend or lover
Lantern (giving away): Vulgarities bring discord in life
Lantern (not lit): Associate offers needed help
Lock: Relief from all anxiety and petty problems

Lock (breaking): Difficulties unavoidable unless cautious
Lock (someone in room): Vexations conquered through hard work
Lock (pick): Satisfactory completion of difficult task
Machinery: Caution required in all things
Machinery (idle): Opportunities lost by lack of planning
Matches: Continuing trouble if not on guard
Matches (won't strike): Unexpected news and good fortune
Mattress (clean): Undesirable offer to make money
Mattress (dirty): Sharp tongue causes grave problems
Mirror (broken): Troubles imagined but can create bad situations
Mirror (face distorted): Bitterness and strife rule
Mirror (face of another): Separation of lovers for a short time
Mirror (face pale): Dangerous things overcome with distinction
Needles: Depression if unaware of surrounding conditions
Oilcloth: Disputes over decisions, loss of friends
Pail (empty): Laziness makes things difficult to accomplish
Pail (full): Hard work pays well, never stop trying to succeed
Pail (leaking): A grand opportunity comes quietly
Pillow (clean): An offer of marriage will surprise you
Pillow (dirty): A barrier or obstacle of some sort
Pillow (torn): Suspicion and envy restrains climb to top
Porch: Difficulty can be avoided by utilizing good judgment
Railings (not supporting): Anxiety followed by regret
Railings (supporting): New and unexpected responsibilities
Refrigerator: A sharp tongue causes great injustice
Roof (building one): Undesirable friends and associates
Roof (good condition): Illness in the family and among friends
Roof (repairing one): Selfishness brings nothing good
Roof (sitting on one): All endeavors will succeed
Room (bath): Advancement in chosen task
Room (bedroom): Early wedding for those in love
Room (dining): New prospects for making money
Room (kitchen): Friends and family make unreasonable demands
Room (living): Dissatisfaction in relations with partners
Room (recreation): Unfavorable vibrations surround you

Safe (free-standing): Comfort and bliss are fast-approaching
Safe (in wall): Don't rely on others, do more for yourself
Sieve: Illness shall quickly strike when least expected
Silverware: Hateful criticism causes strife in marriage
Soap: Loss of friendship over anger and disputes
Spittoon: Someone to criticize you over views
Sponge: Little good luck foreseen at present
Spool: Materialism much too important in your life
Spool (empty): Opportunity lost through lack of funds
Spoon (polished): A barrier must be eliminated before success can be reached
Spoon (tarnished): All plans doomed to failure
Stairs (falling down): Problems caused by misinformation
Stairs (walking up): Danger of position loss through enemy
Steeple: Extrication from all bad situations
Steeple (broken): Many cares over lovely possessions
Table (full of food): Gainful undertakings
Table (empty): Caution necessary in order to accomplish
Table (soiled linen): Satisfying completion of task
Thimble: Flirtation leads to new romance
Trapdoor: Self-deception may create unsolvable problems
Throne: Exasperation over inability to accomplish
Tub (clear water): Affluence and bliss in all things
Tub (dirty water): Caution necessary in order to avoid trouble
Tub (empty): Plans destined to fail for good reason
Vase: An amusing occurrence to take place in the home
Veranda: *See* Porch
Wardrobe (empty): A mixture of sorrow and happiness
Wardrobe (full): Contentment with choice of task
Workshop (disorderly): Success in social arena
Workshop (empty): Prosperity comes after some bad luck
Workshop (orderly): Prospects look better now than before

CHAPTER 18

Miscellaneous

And he said, Hear now my words: If there be a prophet among you, I the Lord . . . will speak unto him in a dream.

Numbers, 12:6

All those symbols which are not included in any other specialized chapter heading have been placed in this section. Among them are found many of the sensations, such as hate, agony, hunger, and jealousy. A variety of colors are also included, as are numbers. Materials such as sawdust and tar are given, as well as a variety of things made by man such as engines, fans, and telescopes.

An example of a dream containing such items was experienced by a prisoner who had been locked up in the Châtelet at Paris. He dreamed, on the night prior to his execution, that a rope was placed around his neck. This was done by an executioner who was preparing the convict to hang. A stranger stepped forth, drew his sword, cut the rope, and saved the hapless prisoner from the gallows.

The very next morning, the man's dream turned out to be

true. He was rescued by some friends who, having armed themselves, broke into the prison and aided him in escaping.

Another example of a marvelous dream which turned out to be profitable was experienced by a shopkeeper in Paris over a hundred years ago. He dreamed he had heard a voice saying: "I have now finished forty years, seven months and twenty-nine days of hard work. I am retired and I am happy."

His wife, sleeping next to him, had the identical dream that same night. Upon awakening in the morning, he got busy and temporarily forgot his dream, but his wife went out and purchased a lottery ticket bearing the numbers 40-7-29. Later that same day, in the afternoon, the numbers came out 40-7-29. The old shopkeeper lamented the fact that he had ignored the voice of his nocturnal visitor and had not bought a lottery ticket. But his sadness quickly changed to joy when he discovered that his loving spouse had profited by the dream and won the grand prize in the Royal Lottery.

Absence (regretting): False hopes lead to unhappiness
Absence (regretting, of friends): Plans to fail
Absence (rejoicing): Shows conditions need improvement
Abundance: Great distress and many troubles
Accident: Care and caution must be exercised presently
Adoption: Small irritations which are worth ignoring
Adultery: Danger from past experiences in sensual realm
Advancement: Great success with some degree of exasperation
Advancement (others): Assistance from unexpected source
Affront: Be wary of false friends who try to hurt you
Agony: Some distress over guilt-ridden associate
Airplane: Ambitious endeavors to succeed greatly
Almanac: Grave peril can be expected
Alms: Secret enemies are out to prove you wrong, if given with hostility, conquest over all if given happily
Alum: Bitter regret over marriage and choice of lovers
Aluminum (bright): A ferocious enemy is in your midst
Aluminum (dull): An honorable position comes your way
Ambush: A difficult decision which affects many
Ambush (if in): Flattery should be carefully observed

Ammonia: Avaricious associates and deceitful friends
Anger: A warning of a stupid but temperamental loved one
Arrow: Greedy associates cause many problems
Arrow (broken): An offer of friendly assistance
Arrow (pierced by): Much annoyance but lots of money
Atlas: Luxury comes at a high price
Auction: Concealed papers prove important
Auction (antiques): Meddlesome friends are in the way
Auger: Powerful foe is a present danger
Authority: Foolishness in business dealings
Automobile: Slander by supposed friend
Automobile (riding in): Very little accomplishment for efforts
Axe: Misery and disagreeable situations soon to pass
Balloon: Harmless games and foolish undertakings to fail
Baptism: Fleeting problems turn into pleasure
Baptism (others'): Great losses of money. Potential ruin
Barometer (good weather): Illness and distress
Barometer (storm): Lack of kindness will bring bad news
Barrel (empty): Everything goes contrary to needs
Barrel (full): Irritation caused by envious friend
Basket (empty): Happy surroundings and peace of mind
Basket (full): Secret adversaries seek to destroy your plans
Battle (defeated in): Irresponsible associates are dangerous
Battle (victorious): Unfortunate entanglements
Bells (alarm): A warning of danger and distress
Bells (church): Persecution of friend does nothing good
Bells (joyous): Bliss and a letter containing money
Bells (silvery): New ventures will turn out favorably
Bells (tolling): Discontent in home and business
Bench (comfortable): Hard work leads to ultimate success
Bench (uncomfortable): Hopes dashed through laziness
Bicycle (new): Desire to do better in this life
Bicycle (riding): An attempt to aid someone in need
Bigamy: Rely not on inflated hopes and misled friends
Bomb: A disaster may change your mind
Box: Struggles prove beneficial, all problems overcome
Box (empty): Except to suffer from temporary poverty
Brass: Danger from too much hard work

Brick: A delay in getting money you earned
Bridge: A favorable time to pursue new ideas
Bridge (covered): Protection from all enemies
Bridge (crossing): An honest effort to change activities
Bridge (falling down): Much distress, oppression due to a lover
Bridge (split in two): Personal progress not hindered
Bridge (railway): Rash conduct creates animosity
Bronze: Evil activities met with resistance of friends
Brothel: Dishonor and disgrace through lack of foresight
Burden: Audacious plans to succeed in spite of opposition
Burden (carrying for someone): Friend has evil intentions
Burial (at night): A loved one will be afflicted soon
Burial (in rain): Much distress but expect aid from a friend
Burial (in sunshine): New opportunities to gain prestige
Cable: Carefully scrutinize offers to contribute
Calendar: Unsettling situation may cause much regret
Camera: The road to success in life isn't reliable at present
Camp: Danger and a multitude of problems on the way
Camp (for females): Beware of anyone who flirts
Camp (military): Despair comes to those who lose hope
Cane: Unfavorable conditions surrounding home and business
Cannon: Heavy responsibilities just around the corner
Cannon (smoking): A secret desire to soon be fulfilled
Carnival: Sorrow and regret over past deeds
Carriage: Old friends will soon quietly visit
Carriage (woman riding in): Sadness and regret over actions
Cask (crawl in one): Many important events to quickly come
Cask (empty): Friend has evil designs on your success
Cask (filled with liquor): Dissatisfaction in abundance
Cask (filled with water): Lack of funds won't hurt you much
Choir: Despondent feelings soon replaced with happiness
Choir (poorly organized): Exasperation due to jealousy
Circle: Never fear when things are really seriously bad
Club: Unfaithful friends attack with ferocious glee
Club (striking others): Poverty resulting from brutality
Coins (copper): Expert to have some small monetary gains
Coins (gold): Sorrowful travel with sad companion
Coins (nickel): Improvement in financial condition

Coins (silver): Much strife offered through animosity
Collision (serious): Danger of physical abuse from enemy
Collision (slight): Opponent may cause grief of temporary nature
Colors (black): Possible demise of loved one or self
Colors (blue): Love will be faithful and long-lasting
Colors (crimson): Censure for illicit behavior
Colors (gray): Little cash on hand and some despair
Colors (green): Great changes and new experiences
Colors (indigo): Estrangement from those dear to you
Colors (orange): Sensual experience to change your attitudes
Colors (red): An angry confrontation in the making
Colors (rose): Bliss in all segments of life, new love
Colors (violet): Abundant study offers hope for success
Colors (white): Bliss due to clean thoughts and deeds
Colors (yellow): Jealous feelings cause grave injustice
Confetti: Disappointment in pleasure-filled evening
Conscience: Gossip will cause some annoyance and trouble
Conspiracy: Misfortune because of unlimited trust in lover
Cord: *See* Rope
Cork: Success in general marred by regretful actions
Cross: Sacrifices by friends bring peace of mind
Cross bones: Scandalous associates use you to better themselves
Crown (gold): A promotion with little more responsibility
Crown (laurel): Prosperity obtained by difficult efforts
Crown (silver): New honors through prudent actions
Crucifix: Indiscretion involves those dear to you
Crutches: Contentment comes when needed most
Crutches (broken): Caution required in everything undertaken
Dagger: False friend soon to attack for no apparent reason
Dagger (seizing): Lies and deceit create no lasting harm
Death: Temporary vexations caused by evil thinking
Death (of others): Care required to avoid grave danger
Debts: Spiteful words are embarrassing to cohorts
Disaster: Loss of money from insurmountable problems
Disaster (escaping): Failure overcome by honest acts
Disaster (rescued from): Helped by friend when not expected
Discovery: Great good fortune and surprises

Disgrace: Be on guard against an attack by false friend
Disgrace (others): Associates try to make you quit
Disguise (wearing): Unpleasant deception to win over others
Disguise (worn by others): Grief and losses by unknown enemy
Diving: Follow your intuitive feelings and obtain love
Divorce: Friend offers sympathy and protection
Duel: Unexpected rival comes to visit and do bad things
Dynamite: Successful enterprise through unique methods
Dynamo: Adventuresome times ahead if discreet
Embarrassment: Distress can be avoided with hard work
Engagement: Opposite sex ignores your advances
Engagement (broken): Criticism in love because of haste
Engine (disabled): Limitations on job offers make trouble
Engine (idle): Take no trips without consulting friends
Engine (railroad): Travel with withered old hag
Engine (working): Pleasures multiplied through effort
Entertainment: Intense pressures turn everything to failure
Entertainment (invited to): Wayward lover sends message
Entrails: Vexation and opposition from morbid associates
Epitaph (friends): Friends will turn away from your problems
Epitaph (own): Pride gets in the way of successful ventures
Exile: Cruelty and misfortune drastically reverse circumstances
Failure: Misdirected energies create financial problems
Fame (for others): Many highly placed friends offer to aid
Fame (for self): Lower your sights and reach all goals
Fan: Injured pride and loss of lover. Marriage will be sad
Fan (losing): Failure to marry the one you dearly love
Farewell: Pleasures spoiled through deceit and lies
Fence: Evil influences warded off easily
Festival: Sadness when older due to sensual enjoyments
File (iron): Selfishness limits success
File (letters): Losses in occupation and numerous annoyances
Fire engine: Some degree of danger coupled with excitement
Flag: Work troubles and lack of ambition destroys all efforts
Flag (carrying): Misery and sickness after marriage
Fraud (commit): Dishonesty is the logical reason for failure
Fraud (by others): Do not invest your cash unwisely—beware
Funeral: A distressing letter or call

Funeral (attending): Misfortune concerning your mate
Funeral (invited to): Notification of a marriage
Funeral (stranger's): Bad news from unexpected source
Gallows (hanging enemy): Progress in spite of terrible odds
Gallows (in darkness): Dire warning of unfortunate happening
Gallows (in sunshine): Success in everything wanted now
Games: Always a good sign unless the games are torn apart or broken up, soiled games denote problems coming soon; *also see* Gamble and Play, Chapter 12
Garbage: Avoid all scandals by being more discreet
Gate: Many new opportunities can be foreseen
Gate (locked): Worry over nothing, security is yours
Gate (stuck): Obstacles are in your way to succeeding
Gavel: Not much financial gain but a nice job
Gavel (using): Friends turned away by false promises
Glass: Tact will be required to overcome enemies
Glass (breaking): Perplexities defeated through censure
Glass (peeking through): Problems due to lack of foresight
Grindstone: Material comforts guaranteed by hard work
Grindstone (sharpening tools): Wit necessary to win
Gun: Dire warning of disappointment and danger
Gutter (clean): Expect stress with few problems
Gutter (falling into): Negative habits create havoc
Hammer: Obstacles defeated through persistence
Handcuffs: Possible jail term for lack of discretion
Harem: Job loss because of sensual desires
Hatchet (dull): Must always try harder to succeed
Hatchet (sharp): Some degree of danger but success rules
Hate: Speedy arrival of sadness from unexpected quarters
Hate (by others): Beware of envious associates
Hearse: Sickness may be more serious than expected
Hearse (empty): Quickly overcome sickness
Hoe: Financial independence in near future
Holiday: Unexpected surprises and good times
Holy communion: Spiritual assistance necessary
Horoscope: A trip with unexpected life style changes
Hunger: Few close friendships will last. Unhappy at home
Incense: False flattery should be ignored

Infant: *See* Baby in Chapter 9
Inheritance: Friends lost due to change of circumstances
Ink: Expect a helping hand from friends
Ink (spilling): Spiteful associates will try to hurt
Instruments (sharp): Professional person will offer aid
Instruments (unusual type): Help will come unexpectedly
Instruments: *See* Musical Instruments
Inventory: A warning to carefully check all investments
Jealousy: Harmony in your most intimate dealings with others
Joy: Exasperating quarrels which bring much harm
Jury (acting on): A small reward for valuable time used
Kite: Pride goes before a great fall
Knapsack: Pleasure will be found in new areas of life
Knife (as a gift): An end of a long friendship
Knife (rusty): Family quarrels and much anger between friends
Knife (shaped like a cross): Danger from attack
Knife (sharp and bright): Friend will be indignant
Knots: Entanglements in business and love require tact
Labor: Completion of task only through hard work
Labor (of others): Lack of cooperation causes serious delay
Lace: Happiness and sincerity in love matters
Ladder (going down): Failure due to a bad habit
Ladder (going up): Persistence will bring success
Lawsuit: Misunderstandings rectified immediately
Lazy: Disappointment over badly done work
Leak: Losses which can be avoided or at least quickly remedied
Leather: Prosperity seen in one month
Legacy: *See* Inheritance
Letter (black-bordered): Death warning, expect note
Letter (registered): A gift of cash or gold
Letter (rose-colored): Lover to write of good things
License (automobile): Opportunity to travel is coming
License (business): Everything to get better shortly
License (marriage): Sorrow for the married and a proposal for a single person
Life insurance: Worry over health will not help
Lime: Success if talents are utilized properly
Linen: Many luxuries and unexpected comforts

Linen (soiled): Complete humiliation
Lock: Success hindered by surprise obstacles
Lock (breaking): No way to escape your difficulties
Lock (opening): Seek new methods of avoiding trouble
Lock (others in): Friendship and love in jeopardy
Lottery: Easy come—easy go; *also see* Numbers
Loveliness: This sensation reveals contentment and happiness
Luggage (carrying): Others create burdens in love
Luggage (losing): Irritations will disappear
Luxury (if contented): Bliss and financial gain
Luxury (if uneasy): Success spoiled by evil thoughts
Lye (for the poor): Honors and some money
Lye (for the rich): Utter disgrace
Magnet: Opposite sex will create problems
Mallet: Unkindness of family and friends
Manuscript: Much work but final success and accomplishment
Manuscript (burnt): New job will be offered shortly
Manuscript (lost): Labor for very little pay
Manuscript (returned): Opportunities are unlimited now
Map: Persistence will overcome all obstacles
Marriage: *See* Wedding; *also see* Marry in Chapter 12
Mask: Folly followed by remorse
Masquerade: Deception followed by illness
Medal: Appreciation of efforts in the home
Medal (lost): Someone is working against your advancement
Memorandum: Allow others to take more responsibility
Memorandum (finding): Expect success through others
Memorandum (losing): Expect financial loss due to others
Mercury: Restlessness will create unfortunate changes
Money (finding): Assistance will come unexpectedly
Money (hiding): Esteem lost through lack of kindness
Money (losing): Rashness will cause losses in business
Money (rolls of bills): Much affluence and prestige
Money (saving): No worry during those hard days ahead; *also see* Coins
Mortgage (giving): Financial embarrassment
Mortgage (taking): Always plenty of extra money on hand
Murder: Great distress caused by a friend or relative

Murder (committing): Regretted actions caused by bitter hatred
Music: *Also see* Hearing, Play Music, and Sing in Chapter 12
Music (concert): Pleasant cooperation from everyone
Music (opera): Influential friends will entertain
Music (orchestra): Harmonious assistance from friends
Musical instrument (bagpipe): Sadness and bad tidings
Musical instrument (banjo): Fun and laughter in all things
Musical instrument (cornet): Stranger will show great kindness
Musical instrument (drum): Danger warning
Musical instrument (fife): Honor must be protected
Musical instrument (flute): Lover will give more attention
Musical instrument (guitar): Lovemaking but far from serious
Musical instrument (harp): Love sadness and recovery from illness
Musical instrument (organ): Excellent fortune and devoted friends
Musical instrument (piano): Harmony and success in everything
Musical instrument (saxophone): Sorrow mixed with happiness
Musical instrument (trumpet): Great opportunity is awaiting you
Musical instrument (violin): Living in peace with yourself
Nails: Fortune can be made with means at hand
Nails (rusty or broken): Old methods with hard work bring success
New (anything causing displeasure): Many things will fool you
New (anything causing pleasure): New ways to gain financially
Newspaper: Beware of idle gossip and misinformation
Newspaper (from another city): Something occurring there of much interest to you; be careful in all dealings
Numbers (one): Individuality and success are yours
Numbers (two): Experience in life will bring good fortune
Numbers (three): The arts will bring you success
Numbers (four): Much ability and material success
Numbers (five): Sharp mentality helps in getting ahead
Numbers (six): Social life and family brings happiness
Numbers (seven): Poise and accomplishment are certain
Numbers (eight): Much achievement but little cash reward

Numbers (nine): Inspiration and endurance will bring riches
Obelisk: Separation for lovers and distinction but isolation for all others, few fortunate endeavors
Offense: Criticism will be strongly resented
Ominbus: Arguments with associates over minor things
Ouija board: Be on guard against false information
Package: A great surprise will come unexpectedly
Package (carrying): Annoying duties must be performed
Package (dropping): Great disappointment
Paint: Improvement over gloomy situation
Paint (spotted with): Malicious gossip with hurt you
Palmistry: You will soon have your fortune told accurately
Paper: Success will be most difficult at present
Paper (legal): Be cautious in all dealings
Paper (wall): Conditions will soon improve
Party (if enjoyable): A new pleasure awaits you
Party (if unhappy): Expected fun will fail to arrive
Password: Influential person will assist in time of need
Patent (rejected): More opportunity in the near future
Patent (successful): Desires will be realized soon
Perfume: Delightful pleasures will pass too quickly
Pewter: Lack of many things and very little love
Pewter (antique): Unexpected source of much money
Picnic (stormy weather): Troubles will overtake happiness
Picnic (sunny): Something exciting and happy to happen
Pins: Many domestic vexations
Pins (for lovers): Petty quarrels end with disgusted feelings
Pistol: Jealousy causes many fights
Pitchfork: Reward for struggle to achieve better things
Pitchfork (attacked with): Bitter, unscrupulous enemies are out to ruin you
Plane: Difficulties will soon disappear
Plans (of building): Expect to soon relocate
Plans (of ship): A long fun-filled journey
Plaster: No long-term success foreseen at present
Plaster (falling): Some disaster is inevitable
Plow: Good fortune in every area of life
Plow (with oxen): Unexpected help from influential friends

Portfolio: Change sought in occupation
Poverty (for the poor): Little change in living conditions
Poverty (for the rich): More wealth will be accumulated
Powder (face): Someone will try to deceive in business
Powder (gun): Disagreeable occurrences happen suddenly
Pump: Success if the water seems clear
Purse (empty): Many things are lacking in life
Purse (full): Comforts and wealth are on the way
Purse (lost): Business and love matters will improve
Putty: Others influence you too easily
Putty (in glass): Results will be unsatisfactory
Pyramids: Many trips to foreign lands
Pyramids (climbing): Distinction but little wealth is yours
Radio (distinct voice): Mental harmony and good fortune
Radio (indistinct voice): Someone is trying to reach you
Radio (shrieks or groans): Dissatisfaction with self
Rage: Remain calm during exasperating situation
Railroad: Many changes and trips soon due
Rake (fair weather): Working conditions excellent for advancement
Rake (stormy weather): Practice diligence in times of great stress
Rape: Dismay over recent tragedy
Repose: Well-deserved vacation or trip
Reprieve: Escape from all difficulties
Revenge: Terrible difficulties caused by merciless enemy
Revenge (others seeking): Make immediate amends for past mistakes
Riddles: Time wastage on matters of no importance
Rope (climbing): A successful rise in the business world
Rope (coiling around you): Entanglement in a love affair
Rope (difficult to manage): Rough times ahead
Rope (handled with ease): Successful efforts toward financial gain
Rubber (flexible): Ability to succeed is limited
Rubber (old and hard): Desires for success are limited
Rubber (punctured tires): Affairs will be delayed unexpectedly
Rubbish (burning): Anxieties relieved through personal effort

Rubbish (scattered): Carefully put affairs in order
Rust: Failure and sorrow caused by serious neglect
Sacrilege: Ruin caused by impulsive destructiveness
Samples: Many funny things about to take place
Samples (for salesmen): More orders are pending
Samples (lost by a salesman): Many orders will be canceled
Saw: Cheerfulness brings quick success
Saw (rusty): Failure caused by ill-mannered actions
Sawdust: Annoyance both at home and on the job
Scales: Ample reward for honest endeavors
Scales (weighing others): Ridiculous suspicions cause heartache
Scandal: Uneasiness created by associates and activities
Scepter: Executive position soon to be offered
Scepter (ruled by): Progress delayed by lack of initiative
Screws: Carefully pay more attention to details
Scythe: Daily duties affected by unexpected sad occurrence
Seals: Secret meetings may bring downfall
Secret order: A distinction offered which has serious obligations
Sermon: Heed the valuable advice given
Shot: Friends will instigate serious trouble
Shovel: Congenial surroundings but hard work
Shovel (broken): Failure to adapt brings failure in life
Silk: Distinction and great wealth
Sneeze (often): An impending illness
Sneeze (once): Happiness and a long fruitful life
Sneeze (others): Unwelcome visitors during the night
Snuff: Friendship destroyed by unknown enemy
Spade: Good profits from plenty of easy work
Splinter: Friend causes pain through unkind actions
Spots: Reputation tarnished but esteem eventually regained
Sticks (crooked): Beware of friend's deception
Sticks (straight): Opportunity for much friendly assistance
Stilts: Examine all offers of advancement carefully before accepting
Suicide: Cultivate courage and stop self-pity
Sword: A well-deserved honor. Safety, escape from punishment
Sword (broken): Dishonorable actions which merit censure
Tacks: Irritation over small unimportant things

Tacks (driving): Opposition and rivalry overcome
Talisman: Protection when needed the most
Tallow: Be on guard against theft of both love and possessions
Tank (empty): No luck in anything attempted
Tank (full): Prosperity is in the near future
Tank (leaking): Grab quickly or opportunity will pass you by
Tar: Enduring health will carry you over all obstacles
Target: Friends and foes alike will attack you
Tattoo: Unusual experiences during a sea trip
Telegram (receiving): Beware of misleading information
Telegram (sending): Asssitance is necessary for success
Telephone: Someone important wishes to talk to you
Telephone (hearing distinctly): Dangerous gossip
Telephone (hearing indistinctly): Concealment of true feelings
Telescope: Something revealed from far away
Telescope (broken): An important event will perplex you
Tent: Job will only be temporary, look for better one
Tent (many): Conditions favorable for success
Tent (with holes): Lack of work and finances
Terror: Prepare to withstand serious shock
Thermometer (mercury falling): Unfavorable for anything
Thermometer (mercury rising): Favorable sign for all affairs
Thirst: Needs not fulfilled at present time. Try harder
Toys: Pleasant friendships and contented home life
Toys (children playing with): Marriage or birth announcement
Toys (broken): News of death or sickness of a young child
Train: Many new and exciting trips to be taken soon
Train (freight): Trips will be financially rewarding
Triangle: Be more serious and develop your mind
Trolley car (overcrowded): Much stiff competition will be encountered
Trolley car (seated in): Security in business and love matters
Trophies: Great effort will bring high achievement
Trophies (given away): Loss of a lover or good friend
Trowel: Embarrassing problems will be solved by strong actions
Trunk (broken): More care required in business and love life
Trunk (empty): Love or business disappointments

Trunk (good condition): Profitable trips will soon be taken
Turpentine: Discouragement in all things
Tweezers: Discomforts changed through very simple methods
Twine: Love and business matters will be complicated; *Also see* Knots
Type: Unpleasant news or serious quarrels
Typewriter: Unfavorable for love
Umbrella (borrow): Loss of a dear friend
Umbrella (protecting): All problems will be overcome
Usury: Greed will cause much sorrow and loss of esteem
Varnish: Deceit and treachery bring much danger
Vat: Associates will cause mental stress
Velvet: Success and distinction in everything
Velvet (shabby): Foolish attempts at success
Vise: Wealth will come through hard work
Wagon (empty): Poverty will befall you
Wagon (full): Efforts will be extremely successful
Wall: A barrier to progress and eventual success
Wall (boosted over): Timely assistance is overdue
Wall (building): Make long-range plans for the future
Wall (climbing over): Progress will be slow but certain
Wall (jumping over): All obstacles will be overcome
Wall (tearing down): Personality will conquer all
Wall (walking on): Security is very doubtful
Web: Beware of all love and business entanglements
Wedding (bridegroom): Successful courtship, few problems
Wedding (bridesmaid): Others will find a mate first
Wedding (by the single): A strong desire to marry
Wedding (church dark): Separation. Expect losses of love
Wedding (flower girl): A marriage delay
Wedding (guests happy): Marriage will be extremely happy
Wedding (guests sad): Marriage destined to be very unhappy
Wedding (in secret): Married outside of a church
Wedding (invitation): News of a close friend's death
Wedding (minister): Others will assist you in love affairs
Wedding (the bride): Marriage opportunity will present itself
Wet: Loss of affection and general unhappiness
Wheelbarrow: Unexpected assistance and many small successes

Wheelbarrow (broken): Self-reliance necessary to succeed
Wheels (idle or broken): Demands cannot be met
Wheels (turning): Financial and love progress
Whip: Family members will be extremely unkind
Whip (using): Extreme cruelty practiced against a friend
Wire: A difficult problem encountered
Wire (a barrier): A serious obstacle must be conquered
Wool (clean): Everything will be very prosperous
Wool (dirty): Application will remove all troubles
X rays: Interesting things soon to be discovered
Yard stick: Unwarranted worry limits your progress
Yarn: Comfortable conditions in all things
Yoke: Marriage and business partnership will be unsatisfactory
Zeppelin (clear sky): Great adventure in store
Zeppelin (stormy sky): War and dissension
Zinc: Excellent business progress in many new ways

PART III

CELESTIAL DREAM DICTIONARY

CHAPTER 19

The Astral Plane

In a dream we may hear a familiar voice cry out in agony—soon we hear of a shocking accident or a serious illness befalling the one whose voice we recognized in the dream.

Gustavus Hindman Miller

Dream appearances of angels, the devil, Christ, ghosts, dragons, and goblins always relate to the moral status of the dreamer. They are very often dire warnings of danger and the need to change in certain areas of life.

Christ, angels, and God seen in a dream with happy, smiling faces presage approval of the dreamer's chosen life style, and protection in all situations. When their faces show irritation or sadness, it is a warning. The dreamer must change or suffer grave problems and much sorrow.

Gnomes and fairies are a good omen. If they appear to be angry, it is also a warning to do something about changing. When a witch appears in a dream, much sadness and bitterness is forthcoming. Greed and envy control the dreamer. When Satan is seen in a dream, temptation is to be avoided at all costs. The dreamer is being told to seek a better way of life—perhaps a new career, a good partner in marriage, and so on. Regret, illness, shame, sadness, and dishonesty are seen to be in the forefront.

Dionysius of Syracuse, while sleeping one night, dreamed he was startled by a loud, high-pitched voice. He looked around and saw a hideous witch, as ugly as one of the Furies, sweeping the room with a huge broom. Dionysius, a tyrant supposed by all to be fearless, awoke in a terrified sweat and summoned his guards. They were ordered to spend the rest of the night in his chambers. He went back to sleep, expecting to again see the horrible spectre. She never appeared.

Two days later, the son of Dionysius accidently fell from a high window and was instantly killed. Within a week, his entire family was destroyed by unusual accidents. According to the historian, Leloyer, it can be justly claimed that Dionysius and his closest relatives were swept off the face of the earth in the exact same way in which the Fury, the avenging witch of Syracuse, had been seen in a dream to be sweeping out his sleeping quarters in the palace.

One of the best examples of dream interpretation handed down from antiquity is reported lucidly by Artemidorious of Daldis: "But it seems to me that Aristandros gave a most happy interpretation to Alexander of Macedon. When the latter held Tyros encompassed in a state of siege, and was angry and depressed over the great waste of time, he dreamed he saw a Satyr dancing on his shield. It happened that Aristandros was in the neighborhood of Tyros, and in the escort of the king, who was

Alexander the Great

waging war on the Syrians. By dividing the word Satyros, he induced the king to become more aggressive in the siege. And thus Alexander became master of the city."

Adam: Everything to be successful and full of bliss
Angel: Guarantee of protection from all bad things
Aura: Enlightenment to conditions of the soul
Awaken: Spiritual understanding is close at hand
Cain: Change your ways to avoid catastrophe, envy will hurt you
Christ: Be more forgiving. Expect mercy in time of need
Dead people (happy): Approval and encouragment coming
Dead people (sorrowful): Conduct must be changed or else!
Dead people (speaking): Heed all advice offered
Devil: Temptation through ambition or lust
Dragon: Faults must be overcome or disaster will strike
Enchantment: Opposite sex will try to cause embarrassment
Eve: Love, marriage, and children born will bring happiness
Evil Spirits: Sorrow caused by evil actions and envious thoughts
Fairies (friendly): Unexpected assistance in a strange way
Fairies (spiteful): Trouble created by a mean disposition
Fates, the three: Serious experiences cannot be avoided
Garden of Eden: Happiness in love, marriage, and life in general
Ghost (black): Great temptation will overcome you
Ghost (speaking): Death or at least a serious illness
Ghost (white): Consolation during a period of distress
Giant: Great courage needed for enormous undertaking
Giant (defeat): Self-conquest will bring ultimate happiness
Giant (to be one): Beware of boastful ways
Gnome: Unusual but extremely helpful assistance
Gnome (spiteful): Great harm brought through mean mannerisms
Goblin: Spite and envy return to hurt you
God: Protection and aid offered as you retain faith
Halo: Great ability to discern mistrust and envy
Heaven: Peace and happiness are yours

Heaven (if unhappy there): A serious lack of spiritual harmony
Hell: A warning to reform in haste
Judgment Day: Listen to warnings of conscience
Magic: Dangerous interference with your life's direction
Monster: Avoid disaster by changing your mind and heart
Phantom: *See* Ghost
Prophet: Reform or be punished by friends and associates
Satan: *See* Devil
Saints (happy): Deeds need approval of peers
Saints (sorrowful): Conduct will cause serious distress
Sibyl: Fortune will soon be revealed by new friend
Soul: Much bliss experienced while growing spiritually
The Transfiguration: Hopeful news through voice in dream
The Virgin Mary: Consolation and cure of the sick. Birth of child to a married woman who has been barren
Vampire: Sexual things will offer great temptation
Witch: Envy and greed will bring harm in many ways
Wizard: Do not try to foresee the future. All is well

CHAPTER 20

Symbols of the Heavenly Bodies

And being warned of God in a dream that they should not return to Herod, they departed into their own country another way.

Matthew, 2:12

This section on dream interpretation contains data for the heavenly bodies such as the sun, moon, and the various planets. Seeing any of these items in a dream presages something unusual and important. Many of these heavenly bodies would not be recognized outside of a dream—except for the color, such as the red of Mars, the white glow of the moon, and certain shaped constellations. The dreamer is given a deep understanding far beyond the usual knowledge of the conscious mind. If you see your own sign of the zodiac in a dream, it simply denotes that you are directly under the influence of that particular planet at the moment.

"In interpreting dream-stories one must consider them the first time from the beginning to the end," reveals Artemidorius of Daldis, "and the second time from the end to the beginning."

There were numerous recorded instances of prophetic dreams taking place during the French Revolution. Each correctly presaged the untimely demise of a noted individual. One of the better known personalities involved was Marie Antoinette. She, as an imprisoned queen, dreamed that she saw a blood-red sun rise. This dream took place on the eve of her execution!

Aurora Borealis: Great excitement created by unique occurrences

Constellations

- **Cassiopeia Chair:** New honors bestowed and unexpected distinctions to gain
- **Orion (The Warrior):** Victory is certain in all things
- **Taurus (The Bull):** Fame through courage
- **The Pleiades:** Lover will be well-matched
- **The Zodiac:** Long trips, fame, and wealth
- **Ursa Major (the Great Bear):** Love and affection protected

Eclipse of the moon: Misfortune, divorce, broken engagements, loss of a loved one

Eclipse of the sun: Great disaster, loss of a loved one, public censure, a child who will become famous

Moon (bright and clear): Devoted love returned faithfully

Moon (clouded): Marriage or love unfavorable at this time

Moon (full): Increase in wealth and new-found happiness

Moon (new): Wonderful opportunities in everything

Moon (old): Decrease in love, wealth, and health

Moon (red): Universal dissension and possible wars

Moonlight: Marriage and love happiness

Night: Evil is working against you
Planets
  Jupiter: Ambition, pride, and success
  Mars: Quarrels, dissension, and possible war
  Mercury: Strange news, deceit and radical changes
  Saturn: Self-control, hard work, and many struggles
  Venus: Happiness in love and marriage
Rainbow: Sorrow will be followed by extreme joy
Starlight: Peace and lovely feelings for others
Stars (clear and bright): A very happy and productive life
Stars (many falling): Death of someone prominent
Stars (one falling): Loss of someone very close to you
Stars (passing clouds): Joy will be dimmed by grief
Stars (polar star): Protection offered
Stars (Sirius or green star): Sick pet will be recovered
Sun (brilliant and clear): Great successes
Sun (clouded): Many problems and much sorrow foreseen
Sun (dawn): Health and good fortune coming
Sun (noon): Cure of illness and brilliant success
Sun (red): A warning of dire danger and distress
Sun (sunset): Achievement unless sun sinks into clouds

PART IV

THE ELEMENTS . . .
EARTH . . .
SEASONS. . . .

CHAPTER 21

Air . . . Fire . . . Water . . . Months. . . .

The witchcraft of sleep divides with truth the empire of our lives . . . However monstrous and grotesque their apparitions, they have a substantial truth.

Emerson

Air denotes the conditions abounding around the dreamer. Gentle breezes are always seen to be good omens, especially for matters pertaining to business and love affairs. Strong winds are indicative of powerful opposition to success. Hurricanes, gales, tornadoes, and other storms of a like nature show numerous difficulties and insurmountable problems.

Fire is to be taken as a warning of rage and discomfort caused by the dreamer's behavior. There is one exception to this rule: A candle flame, burning clearly, presages a state of bliss in both the home and in all love matters.

Clear running water indicates purification and relief from all problems and distress. Rough water signifies much anguish and many perplexities. Muddy or brackish water shows dishonor and misfortune. Stagnant water symbolizes sickness or terrible depression which may ultimately be the cause of the illness.

Columbus heard a voice in one of his dreams. It said: "God

Christopher Columbus

will give thee the keys of the ocean." This prophetic omen gave Christopher the courage he needed to continue his plans for sailing to the New World.

"There is a psychological technique which makes it possible to interpret dreams . . ." offers Sigmund Freud in his *Interpretation of Dreams.* "In spite of thousands of years of endeavor, little progress has been made in the scientific understanding of dreams."

Rich and mellow earth denotes good fortune, wealth, and success in all endeavors. When the soil is sandy, rocky, and devoid of plants and trees, there will be much lacking in life and a good share of unexpected problems. Murky swamps and mud show troubles and shame. This is especially true when the mud is smeared on the dreamer. Such enigmas can, however, be avoided by a change in personal conduct or in environment. Mountains or plains, hills or gardens, when lush with plant life, are positive omens of progress. They are symbols of trying times and misfortune when seen as barren.

Abyss: Danger in business, love matters, or home life
Abyss (crossing): Danger can be overcome by courage
Abyss (falling into): Danger of an accident
Air (gale): Problems and people in way of success
Air (gentle breezes): Much affection and love of life
Air (humidity): Great depression soon to come
Air (hurricane): Losses from unexpected source
Air (soft and warm): Bliss and a lovely future
Air (squall): Many unfortunate events
Air (tornado): Enthusiasm causes danger unless careful
Alley: Temporary bad luck will pass
Aqueduct: Assistance from relatives and good friends
Arch: Great opportunity is awaiting
Arch (in ruins): Hopes are lost for the time being
Arch (passing under): Much distinction and honor
Ashes: Love disappointment and disillusion
Avalanche: A dangerous fall or some great disaster
Battlefield: Opposition will have to be finally conquered
Brook (clear): Harmony and contentment always

Brook (muddy): Passing irritations
Brook (with fish): Extremely good luck in all things
Canal (clear): A very quiet life with those dear to you
Canal (muddy): Serious long-term depression will hit
Canal (stagnant): Serious fever or other such illness
Cave: Secret plans are being made to assist you
Cemetery (rain and neglected): Loss of someone dear to you
Cemetery (sunshine with flowers): A disastrous experience
Cemetery (visited by lovers): Sorrow ends in bliss
Cemetery (visited by widow): Wedding seen coming soon
Chalk: Disappointment and dissatisfaction
Churchyard (evening glow): Peace of mind and freedom to act
Churchyard (in sunshine): Peace after deep sorrow
Churchyard (for lovers): Parting of lovers over trivia
Churchyard (snow-covered): Never give up hope for better things
Cistern (empty): Bliss in love matters short-lived
Cistern (full): Extreme good fortune
City (busy and prosperous): Many great opportunities
City (dismal and dull): Friends and lovers to leave
Clay: Unfortunate sign for making plans
Clay (clinging): Make no new plans for the time being
Coal (burning brightly): Much comfort and joy
Coal (a mine): Riches if willing to work hard
Coal (not burning well): A loss of all affection
Copper: Those in power will try to hold back success
Country (beautiful greenery): Riches and great contentment
Country (dry and arid): Selfishness will bring bad luck
Crossroads: An important decision must now be made
Crystal: Some unique experience should be expected
Crystal (ball): There will be a prediction for the future
Desert: A time of great distress
Ditch: Beware of a serious obstacle to progress
Ditch (falling in): Temporary troubles
Drought: A long dull period in life
Dunghill: Riches especially for a farmer or a hand
Earth (clean and rich): Opportunity for fast success
Earth (dust): Dissatisfaction and disappointment

Earth (gravel): Lack of any success
Earth (marsh): Hidden dangers and veiled problems
Earth (mire): Entanglement in love matter brings disgrace
Earth (mud): Riches and success in everything
Earth (oily): Disgusting disgrace
Earth (pitch): Friends are dangerous and evil-minded
Earth (quicksand): Be careful with offer of employment
Earth (sand): Radical changes cause a lack of success
Earth (swamp): Illness and many other troubles
Earth (underground): Danger; *also see* Cave and Tunnel
Earthquake: Great danger and serious losses
Electricity: Changes to take place; *also see* Lightning
Embankment: A difficult obstacle to overcome
Embankment (crumbling): Insecurity in all affairs
Explosion: Warning not to lose head under pressure
Farm (neglected): Poverty and lack of initiative
Farm (well-stocked): Abundance and health
Fields: Great success and many new pleasures in life
Fire: A warning to beware of haste
Fire (ashes): Sadness and bitterness over all things
Fire (burning): A certain sign of fever
Fire (clothing): Disgrace will erupt, expect a scandal
Fire (conflagration): Personal problem unsolvable
Fire (embers): Great disappointment
Fire (fireworks): Fun and rejoicing over new successes
Fire (flame bright): Happiness in home and love life
Fire (household goods): Mental anguish and sickness
Fire (houses): Great problems
Fire (smoke): Much deception causing ill-feelings
Fire (smoke without flames): Sadness will seem worse than it is
Fire (soot): Quarrels and much bad luck
Fire (stores): Great losses
Fog: Beware of self-deception which blinds you
Frost (heavy): Bitterness over lost lover or friend
Frost (light): Happiness will envelop when thinking right
Gas flame (bright): Extreme good fortune
Gas (dim): Insecurity in everything
Gasoline (lack of): Neglectful ways brings delays to success

Gasoline (plenty of): Success goes nicely in spite of obstacles
Gold (finding): Unexpected good luck in many ways
Gold (hiding): Problems caused by being stingy with cash
Gold (losing): Loss of great chance to make a fortune
Grave (digging): Trouble caused through foolish acts
Grave (open): Losses and great sorrow
Grave (own): Warning to quickly reform
Hail: Expect to overcome problems in way of succeeding
Hail (destructive): Little hope for change
Hill (barren): Little if any progress towards success
Hill (green): Difficulties not impossible to overcome
Hill (on top of): Happy times with much achievement
Ice: Danger is threatening and can be avoided
Ice (passing): Prospects are getting better
Ice (thawing): Troubles will all disappear
Ice (walking on): Caution necessary to avoid trouble
Icicles: Irritations and other problems to come
Icicles (melting in sun): Distress will soon pass
Iron: Oppression getting difficult to endure
Island (barren): Evil associates hinder financial gain
Island (green): All enterprises to be successful
Island (living on): Lover or friend will leave
Ivory: Good luck and fame are yours
Ivory (yellow): All good opportunities pass you by
Lake (clear): Health and happiness
Lake (rough): Much discontentment and trouble
Land (approaching from sea): A very successful enterprise
Lead: Great depression will require courage to overcome
Lightning: Dangerous conditions in all phases of life
Lightning (sheet): Change of residence or occupation
Lightning (struck by): A dire warning of accidental death
Lightning (with thunder): Lover won't leave and crops will grow
Lodestone: Influence of others will help immensely
Manure: Gain in everything
Marble: Wealth but no affection
Mine (busy): Wealth not honestly earned
Mine (idle): Prospects of success are not good

Mist: Act with great caution. Deceit surrounds you
Month: *See* Seasons
Mountain (barren): Obstacles must be harshly dealt with
Mountain (green): Trips to foreign lands
Mountain (on top of): Financial gain and success in love
Ocean (ebb tide): Misfortune and bad luck of all types
Ocean (flood tide): Great success in everything
Ocean (foam on surface): Deception in all pleasures
Ocean (rough): Much anxiety and serious trouble
Ocean (smooth): Journeys and adventures will be successful
Oil: Beware of false friends and hopes
Park (dry and desolate): Bad luck in all areas of life
Park (pleasant): Love happiness always
Path (lost): Faults cause troubles
Path (pleasant): Favorable business prospects
Path (rough and stony): Lack of tact will delay you
Path (winding): Dangerous intrigues surround you
Pit: Great danger which cannot be foreseen
Pond (clear): Security and contentment
Pond (muddy): Some experiences to be unpleasant
Pond (stagnant): Great illness, possible death
Pond (with fish): Good luck and many pleasures
Port: News of a pleasant venture
Port (difficulty in embarking): Complete failure of all plans
Port (easy landing): Travel will bring much success
Port (many ships in): Enterprises to be highly successful
Precipice: *See* Abyss
Quarry (busy): Rewards for difficult labors
Quarry (idle): Hard times for friends
Rain (heavy): Many problems of a serious nature
Rain (lasting): Distress to last for a long time
Rain (showers): Passing irritations
Rain (soft patter): Nothing but good vibrations
Rainbow: Joy will follow sorrow
Road (straight): Opportunity for achievement soon coming
Road (winding): To many irons in the fire for success
Sea: *See* Ocean
Seasons (January and February): Great lack of opportunities

Seasons (March, April, and May): Great opportunities in love and business dealings
Seasons (June, July, and August): Happiness in marriage, luck in love, and success in business affairs
Seasons (September and October): Contentment with many changes, all things will improve, family will be increased
Seasons (November): Peace and serenity unless this month is a dreary one, then it means sorrow and depression.
Seasons (December): Loneliness and depression if dreary but fun and laughter if good clear weather
Silver: Money but lacking happiness
Sky (clear): Happiness and a long healthy life
Sky (cloudy): Sorrow
Sky (rosy clouds): Love happiness
Sky (stormy clouds): Serious problems will beset you
Sky (sunny): Great joy will be felt
Sky (wind clouds): Passing irritations
Snow (dirty): Pride will be humbled harshly
Snow (melting): Grave misfortune foreseen in near future
Snow (snow bound): Insecurities soon to disappear
Snow (storm): Great disappointment
Snow (white): Prosperity and happiness
Steel: Security gained through honorable means
Stone: A multitude of troubles, little financial gain
Strange place: A long, hard journey
Sulphur: Attacks from vicious enemy will not harm you
Thunder: Dangerous conditions in general, personal danger
Tide: *See* Ocean
Trench: Complete safety from danger
Tunnel: A very bitter experience
Tunnel (entering): Misfortune in love or business dealings
Valley (barren): Distressing times coming
Valley (pleasant): Contentment and peace of mind
Valley (unable to get out of): Serious obstacles to success
Village: Bliss and prosperity always
Volcano: Regret and great misery for past deeds
Water (clear): Happiness and great joy
Water (floods): An overpowering calamity

Water (fountain): Life full of love and joy
Water (muddy): Great sorrow and many vexations
Water (rapids): Misfortune will strike
Water (river): Progress in all business affairs
Water (rough): Difficulties to overcome
Water (stagnant): Sickness and mental problems
Water (torrent): A change of luck for the worst
Water (waterfall): Pure and unadulterated happiness
Water (well): Secret meetings with a lover
Water (whirlpool): Involved in many serious things